Habakkuk

An expositional commentary

Tim Shenton

DayOne

© Day One Publications 2007
First printed 2007

ISBN 978-1-84625-055-2

ISBN 978–1–84625–055–2

British Library Cataloguing in Publication Data available

Published by Day One Publications
Ryelands Road, Leominster, HR6 8NZ
☎ 01568 613 740 FAX 01568 611 473
email—sales@dayone.co.uk
web site—www.dayone.co.uk
North American—e-mail—sales@dayonebookstore.com
North American—web site—www.dayonebookstore.com

Habakkuk is the record of a perplexed prophet, unable to comprehend the depth of divine purpose in his day. Written as a dialogue between himself and God, and concluding with a profound expression of worship, this brief book is of great relevance to thoughtful Christians today. We contemplate it and understand the seer's perplexity. Now, to make the book even more accessible to the modern reader, Tim Shenton has provided us with a very helpful commentary on the writings of this man of God. Careful and clear, it is an excellent aid for every believer who would know and love the Lord. Take it and read. And then, bow before the Lord in worship.

James Renihan, Dean, Professor of Historical Theology at Westminster Seminary, Institute of Reformed Baptist Studies, Escondido, California

Contents

Introduction

Habakkuk's prophecy is unique in that it is not a series of messages to the people of God, as with the other prophets, but a dialogue between the prophet himself and the sovereign LORD. Habakkuk does not speak to Israel on behalf of God, but to God on behalf of Israel. He is at times, in his office, more like a priest than a prophet.

The prophecy discusses the confusing and often controversial issue of evil in society. It answers such questions as: 'Why does wickedness remain unpunished for so long?' and 'How can a holy God use wicked instruments to fulfil his purposes?' It touches on the seeming inequality of the proceedings of God in the government of the world, in which the good suffer evil, the evil enjoy prosperity and the worst domineer over the best.

The author

Nothing is known for certain about Habakkuk, the last of the minor prophets of Judah, except his name and what is inferred from his book. His father, tribe and hometown are not mentioned. Some have concluded from 3:19 that he was attached to the services in the temple, qualified to take part in the liturgical singing, and therefore a member of the Levitical families whose duty it was to maintain the temple music.

In the opening he is described as a 'prophet' (1:1), an office he probably held before this prophecy, and which may signify that he was a man of Judah and a well-known resident of Jerusalem and therefore intimately acquainted with the local and political situation. His title and association with music suggest that he might have been a professional or temple prophet. A few have thought he was of priestly stock as were Jeremiah and Ezekiel, and one of Isaiah's 'disciples' (Isaiah 8:16).

He has been called the 'prophet of faith' on account of his belief in the fulfilment of God's Word and the ultimate triumph of the faithful, and because of his extraordinary statement of faith in 2:4 (cf. Romans 1:17; Galatians 3:11; Hebrews 10:38). Some have named him the 'questioning prophet', the Thomas of the twelve minor prophets, because of the doubts and perplexities he experienced.

His name, which was probably given to him as a child, occurs nowhere else in the Bible. It is apparently derived from the verb *habak*, meaning 'to enfold' or 'to embrace' (some say 'to wrestle'). It describes Habakkuk, not as a man who fights with God, but as someone who embraces God and his Word, and then consoles the people of Israel with the assurance that mercy follows judgement. In other words, he takes the people in his arms and comforts and cheers them, as one caresses a poor, weeping child, calming and consoling it with good hope, that if God will, it will grow better. Several commentators say that his name is not Hebrew but comes from an Akkadian word meaning 'fragrant', which refers to some garden plant or fruit tree or to a basil-like flower that flourished throughout Babylonia and that was used for healing wounds.

As with most of the other prophets, a number of traditions have arisen concerning Habakkuk: he was from the tribe of Simeon and a native of Beth-zacar; he was the son of Joshua, a Levite; he was the son of the Shunammite woman whose son Elisha restored to life. This last tradition is based on the meaning of the prophet's name and 2 Kings 4:16, where Elisha says to the Shunammite woman, 'About this time next year you will hold [or embrace] a son in your arms.' He has also been identified with the watchman of Isaiah 21:6 (cf. Habakkuk 2:1), who was sent to look for tokens of Babylon's destruction.

When Nebuchadnezzar advanced on Jerusalem it is said that Habakkuk fled to Ostracine, where he travelled in the country of the Ismaelites. He returned to Jerusalem only after its fall and devoted himself to agriculture. He died in 538 BC, two years before the exiles' return from Babylon. He was buried between Keilah and Gobbatha. This alleged site of his grave was still being acknowledged during the time of Eusebius and Jerome.

The most extraordinary story about Habakkuk states that an angel transported him by a lock of his hair to Babylon, where he gave food to Daniel, who had been thrown a second time into the lions' den! None of these traditions are reliable and they have very little to support them.

The date

Commentators have suggested several conflicting dates for the prophecy, ranging from 701 BC to 170 BC. Some, basing their arguments on a scribal error (or gloss) that changes 'Babylonians' (Kasdim) to 'Cypriots' or 'Greeks' (Kittim) in 1:6, place the prophecy in the era of Alexander the Great, about 330 BC. To support this date they appeal to 1:9, which can be translated 'the eagerness of their faces is eastwards'—a rendering that best fits Alexander's invasion from the west. The text of 1:9, however, is very difficult.

Others prefer the early years of Manasseh (687–642 BC) when wickedness abounded and when the prophets prophesied 'disaster on Jerusalem and Judah' (2 Kings 21:10–15). A third view puts the prophecy in the reign of Josiah (640–609 BC) and a fourth in Jehoiakim's reign (609–598 BC). The latter is the most generally accepted period.

Below is a chronological table of events and their respective dates, which will be helpful to study before discussing, in more detail, the date of the prophecy.

687 BC	Manasseh's reign begins
642 BC	Manasseh's reign ends
640 BC	Amon's assassination, Josiah becomes king
628 BC	Josiah's reforms begin
627 BC	Jeremiah begins to prophesy
c.625 BC	Neo-Babylonian Empire rises to power under Nabopolassar
622 BC	Josiah finds the Book of the Law
612 BC	Nineveh, the Assyrian capital, is destroyed
609 BC	Josiah dies, Jehoiakim begins to reign
605 BC	Babylonians, under Nebuchadnezzar, defeat the Egyptian-

Assyrian forces at Carchemish in Syria

604 BC   Jehoiakim becomes Nebuchadnezzar's vassal

601 BC   Jehoiakim rebels against Nebuchadnezzar

598 BC   Babylonians march against Judah, Jehoiakim dies

597 BC   Jehoiachin is exiled by Nebuchadnezzar

587/6 BC Fall of Jerusalem

539 BC   Medes and Persians under Cyrus destroy Babylon, Israel's return begins

There are a number of evidences in the prophecy itself that point to the reign of Jehoiakim. 1:2–4 mention the moral and political corruption in Jerusalem at the time of the prophecy. The 'violence' (1:2), 'injustice' (1:3) and lawlessness (1:4) of society are in conflict with Josiah's reforms, but they do agree with the days of Jehoiakim, who led the people back into the wickedness of Manasseh's reign. Some interpret the 'wicked' of verse 4 to refer to the Assyrians. If this is correct, the date of the prophecy must be before 612 BC, when Nineveh was destroyed. If the 'wicked' are the people of Judah, and this seems more likely, the date must be put after 612 BC.

1:5 (cf. 2:3; 3:2,5–19) says that disaster will come 'in your days', highlighting the nearness of the destruction of Jerusalem by the Babylonians (587/6 BC). This verse also suggests that the Babylonians, whose activities among the nations were not unknown to the prophet, had not yet reached the height of their power, a world domination that occurred in 605 BC after they had crushed the Egyptian-Assyrian forces at Carchemish. The following verse specifically mentions the 'Babylonians' and their rise to power, pointing to a date before the end of the seventh century. As with the previous verse, it infers that the Babylonians will invade sooner rather than later.

Verses 1:5–11 clearly represent a period before 605 BC, the year Nebuchadnezzar wrested from Egypt the empire of western Asia. Verses

12–17 (cf. 2:6–20) of the same chapter reflect the time after 612 BC, when the might and brutality of the Babylonians had become common knowledge to the prophet. In addition, the temple was still standing (2:20) and musical services were being conducted in it (3:19). From this last point some critics have deduced that the prophecy must have been written either during Manasseh's repentance and the ensuing restoration of divine worship (2 Chronicles 33:12–16), or in the early days of Josiah's rule and reformation.

The conclusion is that Habakkuk prophesied after 625 BC, as the prophecy describes the Babylonians' power among the nations, and before the fall of Jerusalem (587/6 BC), because the temple had not yet been destroyed. He prophesied after the fall of Nineveh (612 BC) (the Assyrians were no longer the dominant world force) and the death of Josiah (609 BC). Habakkuk did not preach during a time of reformation, but before the Babylonians' victory at Carchemish in 605 BC. This narrows down the date to the early part of Jehoiakim's reign, somewhere between 609 BC and 605 BC. (It was during Jehoiakim's reign that the presence and power of Babylon was increasingly felt.) Habakkuk was therefore a contemporary of Nahum, Zephaniah and Jeremiah.

The historical background

Josiah became king in 640 BC, when he was only eight years old. 'He did what was right in the eyes of the LORD' (2 Kings 22:2), instituting a number of religious reforms. Jeremiah says he 'did what was right and just and defended the cause of the poor and needy' (22:15–16). Sadly, Josiah's reforms were only temporary and superficial; they did not change the heart of the nation.

In 609 BC he intercepted the Egyptian army, whom he regarded as a threat to his kingdom, on the plain of Megiddo. During the fighting he was shot by archers. His officers took him back to Jerusalem, where he died (2 Chronicles 35:20–24). After the people had made Jehoahaz king, Neco dethroned him and made Jehoiakim king in his place. For the next twenty years Judah was subject to periodic attacks from the Babylonians until the fall of Jerusalem in 587/6 BC.

On the international stage Cyaxares, king of the Medes, captured Asshur, the ancient capital of Assyria, in 614 BC and the combined forces of Medes and Babylonians attacked Nineveh. Nineveh fell after a three-month siege and the king of Assyria apparently perished in the flames. With this victory the Babylonians established dominance over Palestine. The much-weakened Assyrians regrouped at Harran, 150 miles west of Nineveh, where, two years later, the Babylonians again defeated them. In 605 BC, after the Assyrians had been crushed at Carchemish by Nebuchadnezzar's forces, which then marched west to subjugate Jehoiakim, the Assyrian nation ceased to exist.

Pharaoh Neco made Jehoiakim king over Judah in 609 BC. He was twenty-five. 'He did evil in the eyes of the LORD his God' (2 Chronicles 36:5). Jeremiah accuses him of unrighteousness, injustice, dishonesty, shedding innocent blood, oppression and extortion (22:13–17)—the very sins Habakkuk denounces (1:2–4).

After serving the king of Egypt for three years he was attacked by Nebuchadnezzar, who 'bound him with bronze shackles to take him to Babylon' (2 Chronicles 36:6). However, he was released and allowed to retain his throne as a vassal king. Three years later he rebelled against Nebuchadnezzar's rule, so the king of Babylon, who was busy in other parts of his dominion, sent Babylonian, Aramean, Moabite and Ammonite raiders against him (2 Kings 24:1–2). He died in 598 BC. According to Jeremiah, he had the 'burial of a donkey—dragged away and thrown outside the gates of Jerusalem' (22:19; cf. 36:30). He was replaced first by his son Jehoiachin and then by his brother Zedekiah, both of whom were evil men.

Although the people of Judah had witnessed Israel's exile about a century earlier, they failed to take warning and amend their wicked ways. So God raised up Nebuchadnezzar who, in accordance with the prophecies of Habakkuk and others, attacked Jerusalem. After a two-year siege he captured and destroyed the city (587/6 BC).

The message

Why does a righteous and sovereign God tolerate wrongdoing? How are the divine attributes reconciled with the triumph of the godless? Why do the wicked prosper and rule over the righteous? Why does God raise up the 'ruthless and impetuous' Babylonians to execute judgement on his own people? These are some of the questions that perplexed Habakkuk, challenged his faith and caused him to question God's government of the world.

These complaints in no way prove that Habakkuk was faithless, for from the start the prophet had true faith in the essential goodness and justice of God; but that faith was rudely tried, if not shaken, by the course of events which he knew very well were under the guidance and control of God. What he needed was a steadfast, unwavering trust. It is true that to begin with he doubted and questioned—he was troubled by outward circumstances, struggling to reconcile experience and belief; but by the end of his conversation with God, with his faith soaring triumphantly, he possessed complete confidence in the purposes of his Saviour.

Faith is 'being sure of what we hope for and certain of what we do not see' (Hebrews 11:1). It is the condition and proof of righteousness, the pledge and source of life and the underlying principle of a man's relationship with God. Through all the perplexities and dangers of life, faith holds on to God and trusts in his promises. History unfolds with all its apparent contradictions and absurdities, but 'the righteous live by faith' (2:4; cf. Romans 1:17).

Habakkuk was more a moral seer and a deep theologian than a herald of the future. He was a philosopher, earnest and candid and possessed of unusual originality and force, sensitive, speculative, the suppliant among the prophets and the preacher of theocratic optimism. He was a prophet of justice, not just because he complained about injustice, but because he proclaimed clearly, to the Babylonians as well as to the people of Judah, that man is a morally responsible being. One day he will give account to God, who will judge him according to what he has done. In this way divine justice will be vindicated and 'the earth will be filled with the knowledge of the glory of the LORD' (2:14).

God has no favourites. First he punishes the wicked people of Judah, then he raises up the Medes and Persians to crush the Babylonians for their violent and merciless conduct. He plunders the plunderers, disgraces the shameless, ridicules the mocker and cuts down the murderer (2:5–20). On the other hand, the faithful remnant in Judah is guaranteed salvation even through judgement. In all, the prophecy rises from Judah's particular judgement to the universal judgement upon all nations, upon the whole of the ungodly world, to proclaim its destruction and the dawning of salvation for the people of the LORD.

The purpose of Habakkuk's message is twofold: to bring the wicked to repentance by threatening judgement and to console the faithful by promising salvation. Habakkuk himself, whose dialogue with God concentrates on the overall government of the world, after initial reservations and in the light of evidences of God's power and past dealings, finally submits, without question, to the sovereign LORD of creation. This growth of faith from perplexity and doubt to the height of absolute trust is one of the beautiful aspects of the book.

The style

Habakkuk's style is poetical and nearer the Psalms in structure than any other prophet. His language is pure and classical throughout, uniting both the power of Isaiah and the tender feeling of Jeremiah. It is also full of rare and select words and forms that are peculiar to him. His presentation is forceful and beautiful and his imagery is vivid and sublime. The expressions he uses are bold and animated while his verse is melodious. His style is summed up by saying that his denunciations are terrible, his derision bitter, his consolation cheering.

There is a condensed force and simplicity about the prophecy, in which Habakkuk expresses his thoughts in a few plain words. The diction is always fresh and elevated and at times majestic. The dialogue is direct and dramatic: man questions and complains, God answers and threatens. The lyrical ode in chapter 3 is magnificent and contains one of the greatest descriptions of the theophany in the Bible.

There are a number of references to the Psalms (68:7–8; 77:13–20; 114), especially Psalm 18, and to the lyrical poems in Deuteronomy (33:2–5) and Judges (5:4–5). As a whole the prophecy is organized and clear and, generally speaking, independent of other prophecies, although there are a few instances of borrowed ideas (e.g. 2:14 and Isaiah 11:9; 3:19 and Psalm 18:33). From a literary point of view, Habakkuk has been described as a genius, whose beautiful composition is unrivalled by the other prophets.

The outline

The title
(1:1)

Why do the righteous suffer (cf. Psalm 73)? Why do the wicked prosper and march on unrestrained? Why does God use a violent heathen nation to punish his own people? These are some of the perplexities that confronted the prophet and that caused him, in agony of soul, to cry to the LORD for an answer.

The oracle and the prophet (1:1)

1:1. The oracle that Habakkuk the prophet received.

This verse is the title of the whole book. 'Oracle' (*massa*) (cf. Nahum 1:1) corresponds very nearly in use and meaning to 'vision' and 'word'. It is a burden, a heavy load that is lifted up. It is usually used in connection with severe judgements and implies that Habakkuk is weighed down by his grievous message. It is not correct to apply it to the Babylonians (Chaldeans) and their monarchy, because it refers wholly to the people of God. The prophet is burdened because he announces heavy judgements on the covenant nation and the imperial power, and because he dreads the future devastation of the land.

Very little is known about the prophet Habakkuk. One commentator says his name signifies 'strong embrace' and is used both of God's enfolding the soul in his tender supporting love (Song of Solomon 8:3) and of man clinging and holding fast to divine wisdom (Proverbs 4:8).

The title 'prophet' is used only here and in Haggai (1:1) and Zechariah (1:1), two post-exilic prophets. It is the official designation for a public ministry and indicates that Habakkuk was a man called and sent by God to utter his Word. It is taken by some to mean that Habakkuk was a professional prophet, who earned his living from serving God. This is not certain, although he was acknowledged as a prophet during the period of apostasy under consideration.

The word 'received', or more accurately 'saw', is used specifically of prophetic vision. In this case it probably stresses more the revelational character of the vision than the mode by which it was communicated. Habakkuk proclaimed God's revealed Word.

Habakkuk's first complaint (1:2–4)

In the opening dialogue (1:2–11) Habakkuk addresses God. He speaks as an individual who is pained and sickened by the triumph of lawlessness and as the representative of the faithful in Israel. He is at the same time an advocate of righteousness and a reprover of sin. He communicates directly to God and, in response, God speaks directly to the people.

How long? (1:2)

1:2. How long, O LORD, must I call for help, but you do not listen? Or cry out to you, 'Violence!' but you do not save?

Habakkuk uses a typical lament (cf. Psalm 13:1–2) to express his perplexity—a lament that is not directed against the Babylonians for the following reasons: the expressions used by the prophet clearly point to the evils prevalent in Jerusalem at that time; the whole description is remarkably similar to Jeremiah's account of the state of Jerusalem under Jehoiakim (22:13–17); the four words used by Habakkuk also occur in Psalm 55:9–10, where they refer to internal and domestic wickedness; the Babylonians are not the subjects but the instruments of judgement (cf. Habakkuk 1:6–11); and where 'violence' and 'justice' are contrasted, the wicked are usually the people of Israel, unless another group is clearly designated.

In effect Habakkuk cries, 'How long, O LORD,' until you answer my petition, until you punish the wicked and save the righteous? (cf. Revelation 6:10). 'How long, O LORD,' will you turn a deaf ear to my supplication and a blind eye to your people's sin? 'Not hearing is equivalent to not helping,' reasons the bewildered prophet. He cannot understand why a holy God, whose 'eyes are too pure to look on evil' (1:13), allows evil to remain unchecked for so long and the righteous to suffer so acutely. God's justice is in doubt because his judgement is long delayed. And yet how clearly does God's endurance of evil bear witness to his immeasurable loving-kindness and patience.

The righteous in Judah felt keenly the oppression of the wicked and it was on their behalf that Habakkuk continually prayed about this deplorable state and preached against sin. His cry for 'help' was forever going up to God, for he was like Lot, 'tormented in his righteous soul by the lawless deeds he saw and heard' (2 Peter 2:8). Up to this point, however, his petitions remain unanswered: 'You do not listen.' It is around this silence that his complaints centre.

The words 'cry out' depict a more forceful action than a mere call. They mean to shout or to scream out of a sense of pain and misery. 'Violence' (*hamas*) relates to the continual oppression of the wicked and to the brutality and assaults of those who deliberately injure or murder their neighbours. It may also describe, in a more general sense, transgressions of the moral law and ethical wrong. It occurs six times in Habakkuk (1:2–3,9; 2:8,17), which is more than in any other Old Testament book except for Psalms and Proverbs. It is specifically mentioned as the sin that brought the flood (Genesis 6:11,13).

The LORD remains unmoved, or so it appears, by the prophet's prayers and protestations: 'You do not save' (cf. Job 19:7). He neither restrains the evil, nor destroys the wicked. God's delays often cause his servants to cry: 'When will the Holy One notice and take action?'

Prayers expressing perplexity are appropriate so long as they are offered in a context of trust. Habakkuk's complaints come from a spirit of obedience, submission and love. It is because of zeal for God's glory that he implores God to reveal himself through acts of justice and judgement. He is not charging God with wrongdoing or uttering prayers of impatience. On the contrary, he is pleading with God to save the righteous and punish the wicked. The prophet's design is to ask God how long he purposed to bear with the wickedness of the people. This is the only reason behind his remarks.

Why? (1:3)

1:3. Why do you make me look at injustice? Why do you tolerate wrong? Destruction and violence are before me; there is strife, and conflict abounds.

'Why (a common lament question) do you make me look at injustice?' God allows his people to commit sinful acts in public—acts that are clearly seen and abhorred by the faithful, who have to watch as unjust and violent men rule out of control, untouched by any moderation or punishment. All who really serve and love God ought to burn with holy indignation whenever they see wickedness reigning without restraint among men, especially in the church of God.

The three word pairs used in this verse supply the cause of Habakkuk's complaint. The meaning of the term 'injustice' includes falsehood and idolatry, and portrays the vanity and worthlessness of these actions. 'Wrong' (or suffering) denotes mischief and trouble as well as the accompanying sorrow and wearisome toil. One commentator remarks that the two words describe either the consequences of sin, such as trouble, sorrow, toil and suffering, or the sin itself. Both terms are used predominantly in contexts of perverted justice and social oppression. There is nothing so empty as wickedness, nothing so burdensome as sin.

Habakkuk puts these questions to the LORD for two reasons: firstly, to give prominence to the falling away of the people from their divine calling and their degeneracy into the very opposite of what they ought to be. Secondly and chiefly, to point to the contradiction involved in the fact that God the Holy One sees the evil in Israel and yet leaves it unpunished. This inaction is at variance with his holiness.

'Destruction' (or plundering) describes the open robbery and oppression of the poor by those in authority whose job it was to defend the weak and hopeless. (The word possibly refers to a more general devastation.) Such 'destruction' is carried on 'before' the astonished and sorrowful gaze of the prophet. In addition, there are angry disputes ('strife') among men who abuse the law and endless contentions and quarrels ('conflict') caused by wrongdoing. Everyone is arguing and doing just as they please. All this 'abounds' or 'rises up' during the life and times of Habakkuk.

Lawlessness (1:4)

1:4. Therefore the law is paralysed, and justice never prevails. The wicked hem in the righteous, so that justice is perverted.

'Therefore' not only connects this verse to the preceding verses, but points to the LORD's failure to act against the wrongdoers and to save the righteous as the reason why 'the law is paralysed'. The wicked interpret these times of inactivity as evidence that God will not judge; thus they continue to live violent and contentious lives. The lawful, on the other hand, are disheartened and weakened both in their resolve to fight against the sins of the nation and in their efforts to promote righteousness.

The 'law' (torah) is God's covenantal code established with Israel, given through Moses and set forth particularly in Deuteronomy. It includes the moral, ceremonial and judicial law, and forms the basis of order in God's society. It is meant to be the soul and the heart of political, religious and domestic life. However, the corruption of Israel's civil and religious leaders and the profanity and wickedness of the common man 'paralysed' the law. Through misuse and neglect it becomes numbed and powerless, a dead letter that lacked authority and credibility.

As a result 'justice never prevails'. It is withheld or suppressed by the enforcers of the law, who neither protect the innocent nor condemn the guilty. Evil men rule as they see fit. The government disowns its responsibilities to maintain order in a fair and upright manner. Virtue stands unrewarded and vice is never punished.

The few who dare to uphold the law ('the righteous') are shut in and outnumbered by violent men ('the wicked'). The words 'hem in' actually mean to surround in order to oppress, threaten or bribe. By force the wicked impose their wills on the righteous, who are unable to hold back the flood of evil. The tribunals, governors and judges all twist the law and make it an instrument and minister of wrong. In civil, political and religious life the law-abiding are persecuted while the lawless are held in honour. In every way 'justice is perverted'. How true it is that as long as the tribunal of justice stands firm, the national character is not fatally affected by acts of evil; but when it sides with the oppressor, all hope of reformation from within is lost and judgement must come from without.

Habakkuk's first complaint (1:2–4) is wholly reasonable to the truly religious man. Only the man who believes in one God, who is both holy and good and is at the same time the omnipotent creator and upholder of the universe, has any real problem with theodicy. The dilemma, 'If God, then why evil?' is no dilemma to those who believe in a pantheon of warring deities whose morals are hardly different from those of men and women. But if there is only one God, of undeviating righteousness and irresistible power, then the demand is created for an explanation of the conflicting experiences of life.

The LORD's answer (1:5–11)

The LORD's answer to Habakkuk is in the form of an oracle. He speaks in the first person and addresses a plurality of persons, probably because the prophet spoke not as an individual but as the representative of the righteous. His reply, which neither disagrees with the prophet nor rebukes him, fails to answer directly the question 'Why?' (1:3), although it does state: 'I am raising up the Babylonians' (1:6); nor does it explain the reason for the long delay between prayer and answer on the one hand, and sin and judgement on the other. However, the LORD answers Habakkuk's complaint in as much as he promises judgement 'in your days' (1:5) and a complete vindication of divine holiness.

The two sections are connected by various words: the 'violence' (1:2) of Israel will be punished by the Babylonians, who 'come bent on violence' (1:9); the paralysis of God's 'law' (1:4) will be replaced by a 'feared and dreaded people who are a law to themselves' (1:7); the 'look at' and 'tolerate' (1:3) of Habakkuk's complaint correspond to the 'look at' and 'watch' (1:5) of the LORD's answer.

Watch and be amazed (1:5)

1:5. Look at the nations and watch—and be utterly amazed. For I am going to do something in your days that you would not believe, even if you were told.

Here the LORD addresses the prophet and the people of Judah together: 'Look at the nations and watch.' He exhorts both parties to turn away from Israel and towards the distant horizon and to observe carefully either the judgements that are about to (or have already) come upon the heathen nations, or because it is from there that the terrible storm of God's wrath is going to come. 'Watch closely, weigh up what you see and take warning' is the prophet's message.

'And be utterly amazed' (literally, 'be amazed, amazed'). The word is repeated to highlight the force and continuance of the shock that is felt when viewing such awful judgements. They will be numb with astonishment, dumbfounded by events that surpass all previous expectations. The sight is so horrifying that the very telling of it is incredible.

'For' introduces the reason why they are to 'look at the nations ... and be utterly amazed'. The just and supreme judge is about to perform such a terrible work that even if a prophet of God announced it and described it in detail, or if it occurred in another place at another time, no one would believe it. It is too dreadful. It is too fantastic. It so far exceeds what can be imagined or expected that it defies belief.

The violent oppressors living in Israel are unmoved by any proclamations of destruction (cf. Jeremiah 25:4). Although the Babylonians had conquered other nations, the thought of them attacking Judah is too far-fetched for them even to entertain. 'No harm will come to us; we will never see sword or famine' (Jeremiah 5:12) is their confident assertion. And yet the LORD promises that it will occur 'in your days'. This answers the prophet's 'How long?' (1:2) and confirms that judgement will strike within the lifetime of the present generation. In Ezekiel 12:25, a passage that probably refers to this one, it means within a few years. The LORD's purpose is not to state an exact time, but to bring his people to an immediate repentance. The apostle Paul quotes this verse in Acts 13:41.

The Babylonians (1:6–11)

THEIR NATURE (1:6)

1:6. I am raising up the Babylonians, that ruthless and impetuous people, who sweep across the whole earth to seize dwelling places not their own.

This verse is an explanation of the former. 'I am raising up [or about to raise up] the Babylonians.' The 'I' is emphatic. 'I', the God of righteousness and the controller of all nations, who has been accused of neglecting justice, am stirring into action the Babylonians. 'I' shall strengthen them to accomplish my purpose.

By this time the 'Babylonians', whose capital city, Babylon, had already been mentioned by Isaiah as the city of Judah's exile (39:6–7), had subdued nations and become a conquering people. The reference here may point to their swift rise to power (cf. Jeremiah 25:32). Their rapid ascendancy, the extent of their domain and their equally rapid decline in prominence, forces the question: Who would believe that a virtually non-existent entity could conquer the old capital of Assyria in 614 BC, Nineveh in 612 BC, Harran in 610 BC and rout the armies of Pharaoh Neco at Carchemish in 605 BC? They became the world rulers over Babylonia, Assyria, Syria, Palestine and Egypt, when twenty years previously they were hardly known to exist. Yet their energy dissipated almost as quickly, so that Cyrus king of Persia easily overcame them in 539 BC.

The Babylonians are described as a 'ruthless and impetuous people'. The word 'ruthless' means cruel, merciless (cf. Jeremiah 6:23; 21:7), fierce and warlike (cf. Jeremiah 50:42); while 'impetuous' means rash and heedless. The latter denotes the speed with which they execute their merciless designs (cf. Isaiah 5:26,27), the vehemence and rapidity of their attacks and the hot-tempered nature of their people (cf. Judges 18:25).

Without fear they march on to conquer not only unoccupied areas, but countries inhabited by other nations. There are no lands where their barbarous activity is restricted, no obstacles to hinder their advance; they 'sweep across the whole earth'. Israel will be just one of the many nations they 'seize' and hold as their own. 'Dwelling places' are the houses, towns, cities (including Jerusalem) and territories they possess. However, as they have no legal right or moral basis to take by force what does not belong to them, their achievements, lacking substance, will not long remain.

There is an interesting comparison between this verse and Deuteronomy 6:10–11, where God promises his people 'a land with large, flourishing cities you did not build, houses filled with all kinds of good things you did not provide, wells you did not dig, and vineyards and olive groves you did not plant'. Here the roles are reversed. The Israelites are in a similar position to the Canaanites—they are about to be displaced from the land because their iniquity is full. And the Babylonians, like the Israelites of old, stand ready to possess the Promised Land.

THEIR LAW (1:7)

1:7. They are a feared and dreaded people; they are a law to themselves and promote their own honour.

The next five verses describe the Babylonians in great detail and are designed to instil fear into God's people. 'They are a feared and dreaded people.' The word 'feared' is used as an adjective only here and in Song of Songs 6:4,10 where it is translated 'majestic' and describes the spectacular sight of an army with banners. 'Dreaded' means awesome and terrible and is usually used to describe the awesome response to God by one who experiences his presence (cf. Exodus 34:10; Deuteronomy 7:21; Zephaniah 2:11; Malachi 1:14). Of all nations the Babylonians are most terrible. On account of their gratuitous violence and cruelty to captives, they excite fear and create alarm wherever they go.

'They are a law to themselves', observing no rule or authority, either international or divine, except their own will. They act only according to their own standards and statutes, which they regard as the final authority for both themselves and others. They are a self-sufficient and self-determining people, who show contempt for God and his law. Through war and violence, they advance their own 'honour' (literally, 'elevation');

that is, they lift themselves up in front of others. Their dignity is nothing more than a self-assumed, self-sustained superiority.

The people of Judah have refused to respect the LORD and obey his commandments; now they must fear the Babylonians and submit to their laws.

THEIR ARMY (1:8–9)

1:8. Their horses are swifter than leopards, fiercer than wolves at dusk. Their cavalry gallops headlong; their horsemen come from afar. They fly like a vulture swooping to devour;

'Their horses are swifter [or lighter on foot] than leopards [possibly panthers]' (cf. Jeremiah 4:13; Hosea 13:7–8). The leopard is a wild and merciless creature noted for its cunning, mobility and agility. It has been known to leap seventeen or eighteen feet at a spring. With tremendous speed and power it pounces upon its unsuspecting prey, causing a terrifying and violent death. So the Babylonian army will suddenly attack the unprepared people of God. If they try to flee, they will be caught and ripped apart.

The Babylonians are 'fiercer than wolves at dusk' (cf. Zephaniah 3:3; Jeremiah 5:6). The word 'fiercer' means 'sharp' or 'cutting' (as with a sword). It denotes the eagerness and cruelty of hungry wolves. These 'evening wolves', after a day of fasting, are ready to kill and eat. Hunger makes their senses keener. They prowl and stalk, eluding every trap set for them, until their lust for flesh is satisfied. To the Babylonians the battle is what the seizing of the prey is to a ravenous beast—a savage delight, to which they hasten with impatience.

Their experienced and highly trained horsemen charge into battle, trampling the foe underfoot (cf. Nahum 3:2–3) and spreading themselves in all directions over the land. They 'come from afar' (cf. Isaiah 39:3), that is, from Babylon. Distance is no obstacle to them and it is no security for Judah; for these foreigners, who do not understand the Jewish language, customs and culture, will be as strong and as hungry for blood on the day they arrive in Palestine as on the day they left Babylon.

So swift is their approach and so devastating their attack that 'they fly like a vulture swooping to devour'. The 'vulture' is a scavenger that feeds off carrion (cf. Matthew 24:28). It is bold, daring and sharp-eyed and can easily tear the flesh off a corpse. Hunger makes it dive to seize and devour prey.

The word may also denote an 'eagle' (cf. Jeremiah 48:40; 49:22; Lamentations 4:19; Ezekiel 17:3), a bird of prey with keen vision and powerful flight and that hunts and kills small mammals. It is known to make swift 'swooping' attacks before its victim finds shelter. The eagle mentioned may not be the carrion-vulture, but the great vulture or griffon vulture, a majestic bird constantly visible in Palestine as it circles higher and higher in the heavens and then rapidly swoops upon its prey. Whichever bird is intended the meaning is clear: there is no escape from the marauding and merciless Babylonians, who come to fulfil the curse mentioned in Deuteronomy 28:49–50, to which this verse alludes.

1:9. They all come bent on violence. Their hordes advance like a desert wind and gather prisoners like sand.

The Babylonians, particularly their swift and fierce horsemen, 'come bent on violence'. They approach with only one design: to make prey of God's people and to answer with 'violence' the oppressors of Judah (cf. 1:2–3). The punishment fits the crime. All who live violently, die violently (cf. Matthew 26:52).

The clause 'their hordes advance like a desert wind' (cf. Jeremiah 4:11–12) is difficult to translate and has been variously interpreted. It could be translated 'the endeavour [or snorting] of their faces is directed forwards' or 'the aspect of their faces shall be towards the east', which corresponds well with what follows, that they should 'gather prisoners like sand'. A third possible translation is: 'Their faces shall sup up as the east wind.' The east wind is often used to symbolize devastation (cf. Jeremiah 18:17; Hosea 12:1; 13:15; Ezekiel 17:10) and fits in with the simile 'like sand' and the 'wind' of verse 11.

There are three different meanings. First, the Babylonian warriors press forward relentlessly and in perfect unison. Here is a forcible description of the uniform, unbroken advance of an army, all faces turned in one direction, marching everyone on his way, never breaking their ranks.

Second, the front ranks of the advancing troops eagerly set their faces towards the east (that is, Judah) in anticipation of new conquests. An easterly direction is only possible if the army had already reached the Mediterranean coast and is now turning eastwards to attack Jerusalem. This route is the normal path for an army invading Palestine.

Finally, the onward march of the Babylonians is as irresistible and as dangerous as a desert (east) wind that consumes all in its path. In other words, the Babylonians sweep over everything impetuously, scorching, blackening, swallowing up all as they pass over, as the east wind, especially in the Holy Land, blasts huge areas and sucks up all moisture and freshness.

The Babylonians 'gather prisoners like sand'; that is, they take captives so easily and in such vast numbers that it is as if they are collecting 'sand'. The 'wind' drives the 'sand' into piles ready for deportation (cf. Deuteronomy 28:41). Interestingly, in the Bible the simile 'like sand' is most often used in a positive sense of blessing (cf. Genesis 32:12; 41:49; Isaiah 48:19).

THEIR ATTITUDE (1:10)
1:10. They deride kings and scoff at rulers. They laugh at all fortified cities; they build earthen ramps and capture them.

Commentary

The Babylonians are an arrogant and self-confident people who 'deride' foreign monarchs and 'scoff at' opposing governors, commanders and officers. They hold authority in contempt. They ridicule even the most powerful enemies (cf. Ezekiel 22:4–5). The mentioned 'kings' may refer, more specifically, either to the kings who tried to save Judah from the Babylonians, or to the kings of Judah themselves, such as Jehoiachin and Zedekiah. One of the ways the Babylonians 'derided' captured kings was to gouge out their eyes (cf. Jeremiah 39:7), throw them into cages and then exhibit them to the public.

They pour scorn on every attempt to obstruct their advance. They 'laugh at' efforts to stop them capturing and destroying whichever cities they choose. So powerful are they that all resistance is easily overcome. Fortresses are but a joke to them. When 'fortified cities' are encountered, they 'build earthen ramps [or heap up dust] and capture them'. They make embankments out of earth and rubbish. This enables their battering-rams to reach the city walls (cf. 2 Samuel 20:15; Ezekiel 4:2; 26:7–12) and their soldiers to fight on the same level as the besieged. To 'pile up dust', as some translate it, denotes the rapidity of the sieges and the ease with which the attacked cities fall. The wicked in Judah, who 'hem in the righteous' (1:4), will themselves be hemmed in by the Babylonians.

THEIR GOD (1:11)

1:11. Then they sweep past like the wind and go on—guilty men, whose own strength is their god.

This verse does not describe how the Babylonians passed over all restraint in their merciless treatment of Israel. Such an interpretation is both unnatural and too abrupt in its change of thought from the preceding verses.

'Then' points to the time and circumstances of their advance. After they have broken through the walls and crushed 'all fortified cities', they march on, sweeping over vast stretches of land as rapidly and as irresistibly as 'the wind', besieging, conquering and destroying. They 'go on' in their arrogant fashion, thinking of themselves more highly than they ought (cf. 2 Kings 18:32–35; Daniel 4:30); they 'go on' torturing and murdering victims; they 'go on' overthrowing empires and kingdoms with consummate ease.

They stand as 'guilty men' before the Holy One of Israel, not just because of their overweening pride and excessive cruelty, but because they idolize themselves and deify their own 'strength'. These 'ruthless and impetuous people' (1:6), who were accountable to no one, imagine their own strength, not just to come from a god, an understandable if abominable notion for such a superstitious nation, but to be a god. They refuse to acknowledge the true God, who raised and empowered them (1:6); instead, they worship themselves as the supreme one, the giver and possessor of all power. Self-deification is the most heinous of sins, incurring divine wrath.

There is in this verse an intimation of the cause (self-worship) of the Babylonians' final destruction, a gentle hint at the termination of their tyranny. It no doubt offers a ray of hope to Habakkuk and his people, although they may not fully appreciate its meaning or consequences.

Habakkuk's second complaint (1:12–2:1)

This is the start of the second dialogue in which Habakkuk turns to God in the name of Israel. Someone has commented that it is as if the prophet has fallen into terror by the distressing answer and the terrifying description of the destroyer and has in the meantime failed to hear of the glorious prospect, which was already opening up in verse 11. It is undoubtedly true that the prophet is confused and probably very frightened, but at the same time he knows that the Holy One will not allow his people to perish (1:12).

Habakkuk's complaint is divided into three parts. There is a statement of faith (1:12–13a) in which the LORD's universal justice and holy character are exalted. The prophet still trusts in God despite his perplexity. Then Habakkuk questions the mode of judgement in the light of apparent contradictions between experience and God's nature (1:13b–17). These questions do not indicate a shaken or feeble faith on the part of the prophet, but rather a genuine confidence in the character and works of the living God. Not a weak faith but a perplexed faith torments Habakkuk. Finally, he waits for God to answer (2:1). All is done boldly and with reverence.

There are a few similarities between this section and 1:2–4: the prophet calls to the LORD (1:2,12) and asks questions 1:2–3,13,17), the wicked oppress the righteous (1:4, 13–17), injustice prevails (1:3–4, 13), and hope is expressed (1:2, 12).

The character of God (1:12–13a)

1:12. O LORD, are you not from everlasting? My God, my Holy One, we will not die. O LORD, you have appointed them to execute judgement; O Rock, you have ordained them to punish.

Habakkuk's second complaint opens with a rhetorical question. It is addressed to the 'LORD' (Yahweh), the covenant name of God. This name declares God to be the sovereign ruler of the world, the unchangeable, self-existent one, who is the same in both word and deed and who is actively involved in Israel's history. In short, the name in all its forms proclaims God's eternal, self-sustaining, self-determining, sovereign reality.

O LORD, 'are you not from everlasting?' The name and character of God is the ground on which the prophet's confidence is based. The LORD is not like the gods of other nations, impotent and temporary. He is the 'everlasting' creator 'whose origins are from old, from ancient times' (Micah 5:2). 'Before the mountains were born or you brought forth the earth and the world, from everlasting to everlasting you are God' (Psalm 90:2; cf. Deuteronomy 33:27). He was then as he is now: holy, just, majestic. He is the great 'I AM', immutable in character, ever faithful to his covenants and eternal purpose. On this premiss, how can the Babylonians annihilate Israel, the elect people of God?

When the prophet says 'my' God he speaks not as an individual but as the representative of all the faithful in Israel. 'My God', the strong and mighty one, the great object of adoration, is set in contrast to the 'god' of the Babylonians (1:11). He is the 'Holy One'—holy in nature, in laws, in government, in mercies (cf. Hosea 11:9) and judgements. He is the 'One' who demands purity from his people and who cannot leave the wicked unpunished (cf. 1:13). He is usually called the 'Holy One of Israel' (cf. Isaiah 12:6). The holiness of God is associated with his transcendent sovereignty and power, manifested in the past redemption of his people (3:3).

It is because of God's holy character that Habakkuk, on behalf of his fellow-sufferers, cries out: 'We will not die.' The 'we' points not only to the righteous who are oppressed by their own countrymen, but to all in Israel who are ill-treated by the Babylonians. 'We', as a nation, will not be cut off or utterly destroyed, for God is merciful and he remembers his covenant. The eternal and unchangeable God is Israel's God. He is committed to them. Therefore he will not cast them off completely.

God has raised up the Babylonians, a heathen people, to fulfil his purpose. He has 'appointed them' to be the club of his wrath against the wicked (cf. Isaiah 10:5–6), to 'execute judgement'; that is, to chastise his people so he can re-establish righteousness and restore rule and order in the place of perverted justice and violence (cf. 1:3–4).

'O Rock' underlines the changeless stability and reliability of Israel's God (cf. Deuteronomy 32:4,15). He is their upholder and refuge (cf. Psalm 18:1–3), the sole source of strength, the supporter of all that is upheld. He has 'ordained' and empowered the Babylonians to 'punish' his people but not to destroy them, to discipline and correct the nation he loves but not to annihilate it (cf. Psalm 118:18). He will remember mercy, so that in the end their castigation will lead to their salvation. This is Habakkuk's hope.

1:13a. Your eyes are too pure to look on evil; you cannot tolerate wrong.

There is a marked contrast between 'your eyes are too pure to look on evil' and the prophet's cry: 'Why do you make me look at injustice?' (1:3).

Again, the prophet stands on what he knows to be true. He who raised up the Babylonians (1:6) is infinitely 'pure' in character and unquestionably holy in all his ways. He is eternally separate from sin. His 'eyes' speak metaphorically of his omniscience and abhorrence of evil. He is 'too pure' to countenance wickedness or to look inactively on wrongdoing and injustice. He cannot bear what is morally unclean. He takes no pleasure in evil (cf. Psalm 5:4–5). He never condones but always condemns sin. As a man shies away from a sickening sight, so God refuses to 'look on evil'.

'You cannot tolerate wrong' confirms the previous statement and prepares the way for the prophet to question God's providence. He is proclaiming nothing new, only repeating a basic tenet of Israel's faith in the justice of God. For God to put up with 'wrong' or perverseness (the distress that wicked men inflict on others) is to contradict his own character. Knowing this, Habakkuk is perplexed, for God appears to be tolerating the wicked.

In addition, Habakkuk's faith in a holy God is challenged by the employment of the Babylonians to 'execute judgement' (1:12). Why does God tolerate the Babylonians, who are far more wicked than his own people? How can he possibly use such a nation to punish the elect? Surely the more wicked are chastising the less wicked? Is that compatible with divine fairness?

Why? (1:13b)

1:13b. Why then do you tolerate the treacherous? Why are you silent while the wicked swallow up those more righteous than themselves?

Habakkuk's bewilderment leads him to ask: 'Why then do you tolerate the treacherous?' The word 'tolerate' means to bear with those who do wrong; the LORD does not punish them. The 'treacherous' are undoubtedly the Babylonians, a disloyal and unreliable people, who break their promises and betray their friends (cf. Isaiah 21:2; 24:16; 33:1). The dynasty of the Babylonians was founded on the treachery of Nabopolassar. He employed, in attacking Nineveh, the forces entrusted to him by the Assyrian king for its defence. As a reward, he received from the Median king the throne of Babylon and, after the fall of Nineveh, the suzerainty over Susiana, Syria and Palestine.

'Why are you silent ...?' (cf. Leviticus 5:1; Psalm 50:21; Isaiah 42:14).

Why does God hold his tongue and appear unconcerned? Why is he apathetic and uninvolved? Should he not act to right the situation? The prophet cannot understand why God fails to respond to the Babylonians' merciless treatment of Judah. He seems to sit back and do nothing. The 'wicked' (distinct from verse 4) are the depraved and godless Babylonian oppressors, the fishermen of verses 15–17. To 'swallow up' (cf. Exodus 15:12; Numbers 16:30–33; Psalm 124:3) means to annihilate, to gulp down as a wolf devours its prey (cf. 1:8).

'Those more righteous than themselves' correspond to the fish mentioned in verses 14–17. They are the people of Judah who, though corrupt, are 'more righteous' than the Babylonians. The term may include the nations in general, but the prophet's main concern is with his own people.

One commentator says they are 'more righteous' because, despite their wickedness, the Holy One dwells in the midst of them. Another disputes the 'nation of Israel' view, saying the persons intended are rather the godly portion of Israel. This opinion is based on verses 2 and 3, where the prophet describes the moral depravity of Israel in the same words as those that he here applies to the conduct of the Babylonians. In other words, so the argument goes, the behaviour of the nation of Israel is no better than that of the Babylonians; therefore the 'more righteous' are the faithful remnant in Judah, who must suffer the same atrocities as the rest of the nation.

The helplessness of the nations (1:14)

1:14. You have made men like fish in the sea, like sea creatures that have no ruler.

The prophet's pointed accusation is the natural consequence of God's silence and inactivity. He concludes that the sovereign LORD, who is the governor of all nations, must be behind this massive maltreatment of humanity.

'You have made man like the fish in the sea.' Man was originally created to 'rule over the fish of the sea' (Genesis 1:26,28; cf. 9:2; Psalm 8:6–8). Now Judah and the whole of mankind have been remade 'like fish', without reason or order, defenceless against the fisher's net, fit only to be devoured. The simile denotes the vulnerability and helplessness of the nations, especially Judah, before the Babylonian hordes.

In their impotency they are 'like sea creatures that have no ruler'. The term 'sea creatures' is a name of contempt that generally denotes insects or vermin. Here it refers to the small marine animals or creeping things of the sea (cf. Psalm 104:25). These shoals of small fish 'have no ruler'. They have no organized leadership or government to enforce the law, no guides or protectors to defend the weak and restrain the strong. They are helpless and ready for destruction. God, it appears, has abandoned his people to their enemies and ceased to be their king (cf. Isaiah 63:19).

The Babylonians (1:15–16)
THEIR CONQUESTS AND JOY (1:15)
1:15. The wicked foe pulls all of them up with hooks, he catches them in his net, he gathers them up in his dragnet; and so he rejoices and is glad.

The 'wicked' oppressors violently drag 'all of them up with hooks'. The hook and line is an ancient and widely used method of fishing (cf. Isaiah 19:8). The bait is attached to the hook and the fish bite. The Babylonians used to drive hooks through the lower jaws (lips) of their prisoners and then pull them along in a line into captivity (cf. Amos 4:2). Here the whole race of Israel is craftily drawn together and pulled from the deep, where they thought they were safe.

'He catches them in his net', not one at a time but in large numbers. This 'net' is the common fishing net that is cast by hand into the water. It is a familiar symbol of divine judgement (cf. Ezekiel 32:3).

'He gathers them up in his drag-net' is the third symbol of the

Babylonians' war machinery. The 'drag-net' is a large net. One end is weighted to rest on the seabed while the other end is floated on the surface of the water. It is designed to catch deep-sea fish. When full it is dragged to the boat or shore. These hooks, nets and drag-nets are the king of Babylon's great and powerful armies by which he gained dominion over all lands and people and brought home to Babylon the gods, jewels, silver and gold, interest and rent of all the world. All the major Babylonian deities are pictured holding or dragging a net in which the captured enemies squirm.

'He rejoices and is glad' at his gain and triumph and revels in his own barbarity; he gloats over the distress of others. The two verbs are often used in contexts of worship. Here they depict the Babylonians' celebration and praise of their own strength (cf. 1:11). The repetition emphasizes the extent of their delight and the certainty of victory. All this serves to increase the prophet's perplexity.

THEIR IDOLATRY AND PROSPERITY (1:16)

1:16. Therefore he sacrifices to his net and burns incense to his dragnet, for by his net he lives in luxury and enjoys the choicest food.

Instead of thanking the true God for his conquests and prosperity, he idolizes and deifies his 'net' and 'drag-net'. These stand metaphorically for his weapons of war, military strength, policies, counsel and conduct. In other words, he worships and praises his own power and attributes to the means he employed the honour due to God alone. He is like a fisherman who offers sacrifices to his net after a good catch. These expressions must be understood figuratively, for there is no evidence that the Babylonians offered literal 'sacrifices' or burnt 'incense' to their military hardware.

The forms of the two verbs 'sacrifices' and 'burns' are usually applied to idolatrous worship. When they are used together, as here, they invariably involve pagan worship in a fixed formula of condemnation (cf. 2 Kings 12:3; 14:4; 2 Chronicles 28:4; Hosea 4:13; 11:2). Simply by his choice of words, Habakkuk is condemning the Babylonian practice.

The reason he idolizes his net is because by it 'he lives in luxury [literally, fatness] and enjoys the choicest [literally, fat] food'. His treasures come from the peoples he conquers and his portion is the fat of the lands he destroys; everyone is well fed on the wealth he acquires.

How long? (1:17)

1:17. Is he to keep on emptying his net, destroying nations without mercy?

The question in this verse is similar to the one in verse 13. How long can a just and compassionate God tolerate violence and cruelty? How long can he watch without intervention the merciless slaughter of nations? By his question the prophet intimates that God will soon come to the rescue, that he will sit still no longer. The LORD will in fit time arise and break the oppressors' arm and save his persecuted people.

'Emptying his net' is almost synonymous with 'drawing his sword' or 'drawing forth an army'. Perhaps a double meaning is intended as the sword symbolizes the military power of which the net is the image in verses 15–16. Is the Babylonian king (or nation) to keep throwing out the old fish after a rich catch and then casting his net on the water for a fresh draught? Or to put it another way: Is he to continue dumping old victims in order to make new conquests? How long will this process of filling, devouring and refilling last—until Judah is annihilated?

The Babylonians obliterate whole races 'without mercy'. Not only does this final statement summarize the character of Judah's foe, a hard and ruthless people, but it depicts the pitiless, unsparing and insensitive treatment already meted out by them (cf. Deuteronomy 28:49–51).

The watchfulness of the prophet (2:1)

2:1. I will stand at my watch and station myself on the ramparts; I will look to see what he will say to me, and what answer I am to give to this complaint.

Habakkuk, knowing that only God can straighten out his confused state of mind, pauses and waits for his reply.

Using figurative not literal language, the prophet says: I will 'stand' like a servant on duty and 'watch' (cf. Isaiah 21:6,8; Ezekiel 3:17; 33:7). The word 'watch' denotes either the act of watching or a high place of observation. Some commentators include both ideas. Habakkuk retires to a private tower where he waits patiently and expectantly for God's response. He goes where he will not be disturbed and meditates on the Word and testimonies of the LORD.

Habakkuk 'stations' himself (cf. Nehemiah 13:19); that is, he sets himself down firmly and with determination, unwilling to leave his position until the LORD answers and solves his perplexities. The rabbis think that Habakkuk drew a circle and stood in the middle of it, refusing to move until God had explained to him how long-suffering he was towards the wicked. God replied, so they say, that his purpose was for them to return and repent.

The 'ramparts' or 'fortress' (possibly 'watch-tower') are places of elevation (for looking into the distance) and seclusion (they are usually fenced in). They are situated on top of a defensive wall. Here they display the prophet's attitude of heart and mind or the spiritual preparation of his soul for hearing the Word of God within. They do not signify a literal physical place or posture. Habakkuk deliberately shuts out worldly thoughts and fleshly imaginations and shuts himself in with only his prayers and meditations.

'I will look' attentively and intelligently 'to see what he will say to [or in] me' (cf. 1 Peter 1:10–11). He is like a sentry on the city walls, watching out for danger (cf. 2 Samuel 18:24–27; Isaiah 52:8). Such terms are often applied figuratively to the prophets, who 'see' God's will and then proclaim it to the people (cf. Numbers 12:6). Habakkuk searches with the inward eye. He listens with a spiritual ear. He desperately wants to know God's will concerning the nations, and how he is going to react to his complaint. It is the reception of God's Word in his own heart and mind that chiefly concerns the prophet (cf. Deuteronomy 30:14).

'And what answer I am to give to this [or my] complaint' (cf. 2 Samuel 24:13) has been interpreted differently. Some think it refers to Habakkuk's response to God's reply. God speaks and then Habakkuk answers his own complaint with what God has said. This response may be public or private. Others say it denotes the prophet's preparation to answer the rebuke he expects to receive for asking such daring questions and for making such a strong complaint.

The correct meaning largely depends on the interpretation of the word 'complaint', which either points to Habakkuk's actual argument or to the rebuke he expects to receive for presenting that argument. Some think both interpretations are possible, for the word denotes an argument by which one seeks to establish what is right (Job 13:6; 23:4) and a rebuke or correction by which right is restored (Psalm 39:11; Proverbs 1:23,25,30; 3:11; Ezekiel 5:15). Others call his complaint a speech for the purpose of vindication in a lawsuit and an appeal to the mercy, holiness and justice of God. The word is certainly a legal expression.

Although both the above interpretations are tenable, there is nothing in the verse or passage to suggest that Habakkuk is expecting a rebuke from God. He has not received one before (1:5–11) so why should he receive one now? He has not charged God with wrongdoing. All he has said has been uttered reverently, out of a deep concern for holiness and a desire for God's character and law to be vindicated. There is nothing wrong at being bemused about the mysteries of providence. On the contrary, the prophet displays righteous indignation at the surrounding injustices and a longing to know God's will.

Commentary

Habakkuk is a mediator, who initially questions God as the people's representative. Then, after hearing God's reply, he speaks to the people as God's representative. In this verse he expects a reply to his complaint—a reply he will first speak to himself and then to others.

The Lᴏʀᴅ's answer
(2:2–2:20)

This is the Lᴏʀᴅ's second response to the prophet's expostulations. It is in the form of a vision ('revelation') and includes an introduction (vv. 2–3), indicating the importance and immutability of the decrees announced; a summary of the Babylonians' arrogance and greed (vv. 4–5); and five woes (songs) that taunt the aggressors (vv. 6–20). The whole section is cast as a judicial procedure, alternating between accusation and announcement of judgement. This is most apparent in verses 6–20. For the people of God it is a message of hope, which Habakkuk is instructed to write down for the benefit of future generations.

Introduction (2:2–3)

2:2. Then the Lᴏʀᴅ replied: 'Write down the revelation and make it plain on tablets so that a herald may run with it.'

'Then,' just as Habakkuk expected (2:1), 'the Lᴏʀᴅ replied,' offering direction and information. He said, 'Write down the revelation' in order to preserve it for others to read. A 'revelation' is a vision or message communicated by God. It is a spiritual rather than a physical sight that is inwardly perceived by the recipient. Here it points to the divine communication that the watching prophet saw with the eyes of his soul.

The contents of the 'revelation' are not explicitly stated, although it is probable that the entire prophecy is in view or at least verses 4–20 of this chapter. It is apparent from the necessity to record it on 'tablets' (large stone slabs or tiles) that it compares in significance with the law given through Moses, to which there is a definite allusion (cf. Exodus 24:12; 31:18; 32:15; Deuteronomy 9:10; 27:8).

The LORD instructs Habakkuk to 'make it plain on tablets' (cf. Isaiah 8:1; 30:8; Jeremiah 30:2). Some interpret this figuratively. They say it simply denotes the importance and immutability of the message and the necessity to make it accessible to the whole nation (cf. Daniel 12:4). However, it is more in keeping with the design of the prophet to understand it literally. Habakkuk is to engrave or inscribe the revelation on smooth, wooden or stone (possibly clay or metal) 'tablets' (cf. Job 19:23–24). He is to write it clearly and in large letters so that everyone can see and understand its message.

The prophets, after having publicly addressed the people, drew up a brief abstract of their discourses. They then placed them on the gates of the temple that all who passed by might see and become more fully acquainted with them. When they had been displayed for a sufficient number of days, they were removed by the ministers of the temple and placed in the treasury to remain as a permanent record. In this way the prophecies were guarded from alteration and could be read by future generations.

Sometimes these tablets were set up in market places for the communication of public notices; or the prophet, already in possession of tablets in anticipation of the LORD's reply, wrote down his message on them and then put them in a public place to be read by all.

A 'herald' is someone who bears a message. In this case it may refer either to several heralds, who 'run' to proclaim (or prophesy) the message of hope and encouragement to the public (cf. Jeremiah 23:21); or to the ordinary passer-by, who reads it and then, in a state of excitement, 'runs' to tell others.

2:3. For the revelation awaits an appointed time; it speaks of the end and will not prove false. Though it linger, wait for it; it will certainly come and will not delay.

Having to inscribe the 'revelation' on tablets suggests that its fulfilment is still some way off. What the prophet sees and foretells 'awaits an appointed time'; that is, the period of its accomplishment, although not immediately at hand, has been fixed and determined by God (cf. Daniel 10:14; 11:27,35).

'Speaks' is not a good translation. The word means either to transpire and breathe out, or to pant and hasten. The former depicts the revelation as a lifeless body that is resurrected at the appointed time; the latter shows it striving to fulfil itself and panting to reach its goal. It may be that the prophecy is here personified, as it goes on vigorously and struggles, as it were, with a certain vehemence, yearning for its accomplishment and fulfilment. The prophecy itself gasps for the 'end'. The term 'end' denotes a termination point. Here it signifies the end of the waiting time, the end of the Babylonian oppression and the fulfilment of God's Word.

The revelation 'will not prove false'. It will not lie or deceive like the predictions of false prophets. It will not frustrate the expectations it has encouraged. A 'herald' can 'run' to proclaim it, for it will not disappoint. Though it tarries and causes anxiety, 'wait for it'. Be faithful and hopeful. Be patient and allow God to act in his own way and time, for 'it will certainly come' to pass. It will not be postponed or arrive even a day after the appointed time. God's Word is never late and his delays are always wise.

The Septuagint changes the gender: 'Though he linger, wait for him; he will certainly come and will not delay.' This has caused a number of commentators to apply the verse to the coming of the Messiah. To support their argument they refer to Hebrews 10:36–37, where, in connection with Isaiah 26:20, this verse is quoted. The writer to the Hebrews, however, is not interpreting Habakkuk 2:3 strictly. He is rather applying its message of patience to the weary and suffering

Christians of his day, who were waiting for Christ to fulfil his promises and to judge their enemies.

The Babylonians (2:4–5)

THEIR ARROGANCE (2:4–5A)

2:4. See, he is puffed up; his desires are not upright—but the righteous will live by his faith—

The prophecy itself begins in this verse, which answers the moral problem set in 1:13. 'See,' or behold, introduces the revelation and exhorts the prophet to take special notice of it. The hearts and minds of the Babylonian oppressors are 'puffed up' (literally, 'swollen'). They are swollen with pride and bloated with self-glorification. In all they do, they act haughtily and presumptuously, exalting themselves above God (cf. 1:11) and seeking only their own ends. They are self-reliant and insolent people, who regard themselves as indestructible and as the sole source of righteousness.

The appetites or souls ('desires') of the Babylonians are not morally 'upright'. To be upright is to be straight or level (cf. Isaiah 26:7), to live without turning or trickery. The Babylonians are crooked and uneven in behaviour, perverted and corrupt in character. Their wickedness, which God abhors, will lead ultimately to judgement and death.

The LORD immediately introduces a contrasting thought to the behaviour and fate of the wicked—'the righteous will live by his faith'. The Talmud declares that this one statement encapsulates the 613 laws of the Pentateuch. It is also a summary of the Old Testament way to salvation and the key to Paul's doctrinal teaching (cf. Romans 1:7; Galatians 3:11; Hebrews 10:38). However, it is not the central message of Habakkuk's book.

The 'righteous' are the just and humble who 'live' by the constancy of their faith. 'Faith' here denotes firmness and steadfastness (cf. Isaiah 7:9), the way in which a person continues to live, rather than the way in which he is to be justified. It is a faith that strips us of all arrogance and leads us naked and needy to God, that we may seek salvation from him alone. Just as a building is established on its foundations or a tree by its roots, so the man of faith stands without wavering on God.

As an attribute of God 'faith' means trustworthiness, unchangeable fidelity in the fulfilment of his promises; as a personal attribute of man, it speaks of fidelity in word and deed; and, in his relation to God, firm attachment to God, an undisturbed confidence in the divine promises of grace. The latter is the primary sense in this passage. The man of faith adheres lovingly to God, believes wholeheartedly in his Word and waits in patient assurance for him to act. The righteous man, however baffled his faith is by experience, holds on in loyalty to God and duty.

The LXX (Septuagint) reads: 'The just by my [God's] faithfulness shall live.' In other words, the faithfulness is on God's part, life coming because God, through his covenant, promises to preserve his people. This is a less natural interpretation.

In contrast to the imminent national demise of the oppressor, the righteous in Judah will 'live'. A remnant will be saved from destruction on the condition that they retain their trust in God. One writer comments that despite the approaching judgement God will vindicate his people by giving them life, both temporally and eschatologically. In this context the life promised is political and national. The verse could be summed up by saying that the justified by faith continue to live by faith. Despite the just judgements of God, a remnant will survive; they will live by exercising a steadfast trust through the darkest hours.

2:5a. indeed, wine betrays him; he is arrogant and never at rest.

This verse carries on from verse 4a, applying it to the Babylonians. The

Babylonians' desire for expansion and conquest, picked up from 1:15–17, is further elaborated and condemned in 2:6–17. This verse therefore serves as a transition to the next part of God's message to Habakkuk. For the present the wicked continue on their brutal and prosperous way, and yet, without realizing, they are marching ever closer to judgement and doom.

'Furthermore' is a better translation than 'indeed' as the verse follows on from 4a. 'Wine betrays him.' The 'puffed up' (2:4) Babylonians were notorious for their drinking habits (cf. Jeremiah 51:7). It is well known, for instance, that the city of Babylon was conquered while King Belshazzar and his nobles were feasting and drinking wine (Daniel 5:1ff.). In the present context 'wine' denotes, not only the excesses and vices of the Babylonians, but the deceiving power of alcoholic liquor. 'Wine' robs a man of his senses and powers of judgement, blinding him to his true condition. It inflames pride and causes expressions of bloated self-esteem to flow from the drunkard's lips. (cf. 2:4a). Instead of bringing strength, as the drinker imagines, wine opens the door to destruction; it 'betrays' (cf. Proverbs 23:29–35).

In short, the LORD compares the proud to drunken men, who, forgetting all reason and shame, abandon themselves to all that is disgraceful; for the drunkard distinguishes nothing and becomes like a brute animal, so that he shuns nothing that is base and unbecoming. Understood figuratively, the Babylonians are intoxicated with power and dominion. Success has swollen and befuddled their heads.

Encouraged by wine, the Babylonians are insolent and loud-mouthed ('arrogant') and 'never at rest'. The latter phrase indicates the restlessness of ambition. Ambitious men cannot abide at home or remain settled and content, for a lust for power drives them abroad, where they fight and conquer. Like drunkards, who are unable to restrain themselves, the Babylonians find pleasure in going forth to destroy.

THEIR GREED (2:5B)

2:5b. Because he is as greedy as the grave and like death is never satisfied, he gathers to himself all the nations and takes captive all the peoples.

'He is as greedy as the grave.' He possesses an insatiable desire to open wide his mouth and devour all (cf. Isaiah 5:14). Just as the grave (*sheol*), the place of the dead, swallows every living thing and yet remains hungry, yearning for more, so the Babylonians are 'never satisfied' (cf. Proverbs 27:20; 30:15–16; Habakkuk 1:15–17). 'Death' is personified to add force to the fact that though sparing none, the Babylonians' appetite never says, 'Enough!'

So intent is he on fulfilling his desires that he quickly 'gathers' or adds to his kingdom, one after another, all the surrounding 'nations', just as a farmer collects grain from his fields at harvest time. Then he deports thousands of prisoners to his own land. There is no moderation shown by the arrogant, drunken Babylonians, whose wickedness spurs on their approaching destruction.

The first woe against the Babylonians (2:6–8)

The whole passage (verses 6–20) is a fivefold taunt-song delivered by the nations against the Babylonians. Each 'woe', or mocking statement, consists of three verses. These verses describe not only some specific (and habitual) crime of the Babylonians, but their appropriate punishment as well.

THEIR EXTORTION (2:6)

2:6. Will not all of them taunt him with ridicule and scorn, saying, 'Woe to him who piles up stolen goods and makes himself wealthy by extortion! How long must this go on?'

The opening is put in the form of a question to make it more forceful. 'All of them' refers back to 'all the nations and ... all the peoples' of the previous verse. They are the nations that have been conquered and ill-treated by the Babylonians, and the peoples who eagerly wait for God's wrath to fall on their oppressors.

The prophet employs three words to describe the dirge. The first is 'taunt' (*mashal*), which is a type of proverb or pithy sentence that is used to ridicule others. It sometimes denotes a parable or allegory (a figurative discourse), or even a mocking byword. The second word is 'ridicule' (*melisah*) (cf. Proverbs 1:6), which signifies a scoff or a taunt by which any one is reproved. It comes from another word (*lis*) meaning 'to scorn, to deride, to laugh at'. Some say it is an ambiguous or enigmatic discourse that requires interpretation. Others think it is an explanatory saying. The latter meanings do not suit the passage as well.

The third word 'scorn' (*hidot*) is a riddle or an obscure saying. It is obscure or dark because it refers to a judgement that is so far indiscernible to human sense. According to one writer it is a taunting song in the form of riddles. The real meaning is skilfully hidden, or at least obscured, by using words that have a twofold sense. The intended meaning is brought out by emphasizing certain words or by accompanying the words with a significant look or gesture, or the meaning only becomes apparent after careful study.

The three words are more often used in wisdom literature and teaching; therefore Babylonia serves here as a proverbial kind of object lesson of those who overstep God's bounds.

The prophets commonly use the interjection 'woe' (cf. 2:9, 12, 15, 19; Isaiah 5) to introduce divine judgements. It is also used in funeral dirges. Here it prefixes the miseries that will come upon the Babylonians, 'who pile up stolen goods'. By fraud, robbery and oppression the Babylonians amass countless treasures that do not belong to them; they heap up the possessions of others in order to carry them to their own homes.

'And makes himself wealthy by extortion!' The noun 'extortion' (*abtit*) means either a heap of clay or thick mud or a heavy pledge. The former depicts a load of guilt or a mass of dirt that the Babylonians heap on themselves to their own destruction. The Babylonians are weighed down by a multitude of worldly possessions and by the sin they commit to require them.

The latter meaning, a mass of pledges, is more in keeping with the context of the passage. Pledges are items used as security by a creditor in case of default on a loan. They were exacted from debtors contrary to the law of Moses (Deuteronomy 24:10–13) and their accumulation often led to the exploitation and enslavement of the poor (cf. 2 Kings 4:1–2; Nehemiah 5:1–13). The phrase denotes either that the 'wealth' of the Babylonians is acquired from unjust and illegal pledges, which are therefore reclaimable by the extorted; or that they collect the property of the nations just as the unmerciful usurer heaps up pledges. In so acting they pile up their debt to God.

'How long must this go on [with impunity]' are the sighs of the oppressed, who are experiencing firsthand the heinousness of this extortion. According to them the wicked have survived long enough. 'When will the plundering stop?' is their shocked cry. 'How long will God watch and not judge?' The implication of this protestation is that one day retribution will overtake the perpetrators.

THEIR OVERTHROW (2:7–8)

2:7. Will not your debtors suddenly arise? Will they not wake up and make you tremble? Then you will become their victim.

Some translate the word 'debtors' as 'biters' and apply it to the savage bites of vipers (cf. Jeremiah 8:17). These serpents, as instruments of God's wrath, will devour the Babylonians. The more natural meaning of the word is creditors, men who exact usurious interest from debtors. They are the extorted poor of verse 6b and the 'peoples who are left' of verse 8. When the extortion becomes unbearable, these former debtors will 'suddenly' and unexpectedly 'arise' to their feet in revolt; they will become creditors, exacting money with heavy interest from the Babylonians.

They will 'wake up and make you tremble'. Just as the Babylonians seized their debtors and mercilessly exacted payment from them, so these tormentors will stir themselves from their sleep of fear and shake the Babylonians, demanding back what had been stolen. Those who had made others tremble will themselves tremble.

'Then you will become their victim' (cf. Jeremiah 50:10). The Babylonians, who have accumulated vast amounts of booty from many nations, will be plundered by those nations. In a reversal of roles, the spoiler will be spoiled. Former victims of the Babylonians, the Medes and Persians, whose sudden rise to power resembled that of the Babylonian Empire, carried this sentence out less than twenty-five years after Nebuchadnezzar's death.

2:8. Because you have plundered many nations, the peoples who are left will plunder you. For you have shed man's blood; you have destroyed lands and cities and everyone in them.

Here is the reason for the 'woe' just announced: 'Because [or for] you have plundered many nations' (cf. Jeremiah 25:9; 27:6). The Babylonians have sacked cities; slain, enslaved and deported their inhabitants; stolen their treasures and deposed their kings. 'The peoples who are left' may include the nations the Babylonians did not plunder, but it mainly refers to the survivors (the remnant) within the conquered nations. Specifically, it points to the Medes and Persians who had been attacked and spoiled by Nebuchadnezzar. These 'peoples' will 'plunder' Babylon by violence and usury (cf. Jeremiah 50:10).

Today the site of Babylon is a desolate waste, with the caves and holes in the ruins occupied only by wild animals of the desert: lions, jackals and various other animals that sport among the ruins and whose cries re-echo through the caverns of the ancient palace walls. Human beings are seldom seen in the vicinity.

By invading foreign lands and by treating their victims so mercilessly, the Babylonians have shed innocent 'blood'. Through oppression and injustice they have 'destroyed lands and cities and everyone in them'. This not only points to Judah, Jerusalem and her inhabitants, but to all the lands they have ravaged, to all the cities they have pillaged and burned, and to all the occupants they have slaughtered or deported. In Jeremiah, Babylon is rightly called 'the hammer of the whole earth' (50:23), and the LORD's 'war club, my weapon for battle—with you I shatter nations, with you I destroy kingdoms' (51:20).

The second woe against the Babylonians (2:9–11)

The second woe concerns the Babylonians' attempt to dominate the nations; it condemns their deliberate exploitation for personal and dynastic gain.

THEIR INJUSTICE AND CRUELTY (2:9)

2:9. Woe to him who builds his realm by unjust gain to set his nest on high, to escape the clutches of ruin!

Woe to the guilty tyrant who establishes 'his realm by unjust [evil] gain'. 'Realm' refers to the Babylonian dynasty, although it could apply to the commoner's family line. 'Unjust gain' depicts the sinful covetousness, rapacity and plundering of the Babylonians, who build their kingdom with the spoils of conquered nations. It highlights their love of illegal gain and greedy profiteering.

'To set his nest on high' (cf. Numbers 24:21; Jeremiah 49:16; Obadiah 4) is an allusion to the eagle that builds its nest in inaccessible places among the rocks (cf. Job 39:27). From there it watches and swoops down on its prey (cf. 1:8). Like the eagle, the Babylonians, although occupying low-lying country, make their 'nest on high'; that is, from the wealth of others they construct huge fortifications that provide invulnerable security.

From this elevated position they regard themselves as higher than God, outside his justice and beyond 'the clutches of ruin [evil]'. They imagine that it is impossible for the hand of adversity to reach them and for a hostile fate to fasten itself onto them. They are secure from all dangers below. Therefore sovereignty will never be wrested from their family; they will reign for ever. Apparently, Nebuchadnezzar's life's goal was to establish an illustrious, lasting dynasty and to make an everlasting name for his reign.

How futile are lofty and arrogant thoughts! A man reaps what he sows. 'You said in your heart, "I will ascend to heaven; I will raise my throne above the stars of God" ... but you are brought down to the grave, to the depths of the pit' (Isaiah 14:12–17).

THEIR SHAME AND RUIN (2:10–11)

2:10. You have plotted the ruin of many peoples, shaming your own house and forfeiting your life.

The Babylonians have 'plotted the ruin' or rather cut off and annihilated 'many peoples'. They have enslaved and destroyed whole races of men and impoverished entire cities and nations. And yet, instead of reaping riches, honour and glory, they have brought disgrace to their own dynasty ('house'), for which these cruelties and injustices were committed. Shame and ruin are the only rewards for shedding innocent blood.

'And forfeiting your life' can also be translated 'and sinning against your soul'. The verb 'forfeit' conveys the idea of being at fault due to some lack and its resultant guilt. The phrase means either to throw away your life by wicked conduct or to bring retribution on yourself by sinning against your own soul. In others words, the Babylonians are jeopardizing their own lives by seeking to destroy others. The evils they have perpetrated on 'many peoples' are returning on their own heads.

2:11. The stones of the wall will cry out, and the beams of the woodwork will echo it.

The 'stones of the [outside] wall' of houses and palaces that have been built by plunder and cruelty will 'cry out' to God for vengeance. They will moan in agony because of the evil practised to construct them. As witnesses they will lift their voices to accuse the guilty and to protest at the injustice of the wicked (cf. 1:2–3; Genesis 4:10; Luke 19:40).

'The beams of the woodwork will echo' the cry of the stones. These wooden tie beams or rafters were placed in the middle of buildings to hold the walls together. Here they may denote the upper rooms of the palace that will 'echo' or confirm the charges uttered by the stones. Each part of the building will bear witness to the crimes of the builder. Inanimate objects will join together, in a chorus of condemnation, to sing out against the bloodshed and fraud of the Babylonians.

The third woe against the Babylonians (2:12–14)
THEIR VIOLENCE (2:12)
2:12. Woe to him who builds a city with bloodshed and establishes a town by crime!

The Babylonians are charged with ruthless self-aggrandizement. The huge fortifications (the walls surrounding Babylon measured between seventeen and twenty-two metres in width—the normal thickness of a city wall was three to seven metres) and magnificent buildings of

Babylonia and its capital are cemented together with the blood of innocent victims (cf. Micah 3:10). Murder, cruelty, oppression, tyranny of every kind—these are the foundation stones on which Babylon's empire and society are built. But 'woe to him' who destroys other cities and civilizations in order to construct his own metropolis. 'Woe to him' who plunders the property of foreigners and uses slave labour to upgrade his own kingdom. 'Woe to him' who 'establishes a town by [the] crime' of extortion. He will be destroyed without remedy.

THEIR DESTRUCTION (2:13)

2:13. Has not the LORD Almighty determined that the people's labour is only fuel for the fire, that the nations exhaust themselves for nothing?

The prophet calls for attention and proclaims the divine origin of Babylon's destruction. The title 'LORD Almighty' or literally 'LORD of armies' expresses God's sovereign rule as king and commander over every created force. It is often associated, as here, with his militant judgement of enemies—a judgement that is executed on behalf of his own people.

God is not unconcerned, for he has willed and ordered ('determined') that 'the people's labour is only fuel for the fire'. To construct a city and an empire for self-aggrandizement is pointless, for both the effort and the achievement possess no lasting value. Such kingdoms are built only to be consumed by fire (cf. Genesis 19:24–25; Deuteronomy 9:3; Isaiah 1:7; Amos 2:5), prepared only to be destroyed; they literally go up in smoke. The 'people' are the slaves used by the Babylonians as well as the Babylonians themselves.

The 'nations', particularly Babylonia (the term includes nations from every generation), spend their strength and life in vain. They 'exhaust themselves' in order to obtain what is profitless and to preserve what they cannot keep. It is 'a chasing after the wind' (Ecclesiastes 2:17), a work of emptiness and nothingness. The prophet Jeremiah borrows (or echoes) this verse and applies it specifically to Babylon: 'Babylon's thick wall will be levelled and her high gates set on fire; the peoples exhaust themselves for nothing, the nations' labour is only fuel for the flames' (51:58).

THE GLORY OF THE LORD (2:14)

2:14. For the earth will be filled with the knowledge of the glory of the LORD, as the waters cover the sea.

The destruction of the Babylonians, with their godless systems and arrogant autonomy, will pave the way for 'the earth' to be 'filled with the knowledge of the glory of the LORD' (cf. Numbers 14:21; Isaiah 6:3). 'The earth' points to Judah in particular and to all the lands oppressed by the Babylonians in general. Just as the tabernacle and temple were filled with the glory of the LORD (cf. Exodus 40:34; 1 Kings 8:11), so the whole earth will be covered with the sight and sense of God's splendour.

When the Babylonians are crushed, all the inhabitants of the earth will acknowledge God's power and the awesomeness of his presence; through the extermination of evildoers they will obtain a 'knowledge' of his righteousness and declare that the world is governed solely by his hand. The 'glory of the LORD' is the sovereign majesty, the absolute dominion and the matchless power of God, manifested in the judgements of ungodly powers. 'As the waters [spread and] cover the [bottom of the] sea' denotes an overflowing abundance. The knowledge of the glory of the LORD will spread throughout the earth, saturating every land.

Some commentators, following on from Isaiah 11:9, interpret verse 14 either Messianically or eschatologically. They apply it either to the first advent of Christ, when the knowledge of God's glory filled the earth; to the last days, when God will move powerfully and bring his kingdom to all creation; or to the consummation of all things, when the Messiah will return in triumph and glory to judge both the living and the dead, and to establish his universal and eternal kingdom.

Commentary

Little objection can be raised if the meaning of verse 14 is extended to include the above. However, an important distinction must be made between Habakkuk 2:14 and Isaiah 11:9. The latter closes the description of the glory and blessedness of the Messianic kingdom in its perfected state. The earth is then full of the knowledge of the LORD. Habakkuk, on the other hand, describes the outcome of God's judgement of the Babylonians: that the earth will be filled, not so much with the knowledge of the LORD, but with the knowledge of his glory.

The fourth woe against the Babylonians (2:15–17)

The fourth woe describes the Babylonians' cruel treatment of the nations they conquered as well as their own appropriate punishment.

THEIR OPPRESSION (2:15)

2:15. Woe to him who gives drink to his neighbours, pouring it from the wineskin till they are drunk, so that he can gaze on their naked bodies.

In view of 2:5, it is not surprising that many commentators refer this verse to the excessive drinking habits of the Babylonians and to their practice of giving intoxicating and sometimes poisonous liquor to neighbouring nations as a mark of feigned friendship; for they revelled not only in deceiving others, but in involving them in their own debauchery, lust and uncleanness.

The language of the verse, however, is more figurative than literal (cf. 2:16). The figure, suggested by the habits of the Babylonians (2:5), is taken from ordinary life, where one man gives another a drink so as to intoxicate him, for the purpose of indulging his own wantonness at his neighbour's expense or of taking delight in his shame. The Babylonians made other nations 'drunk' in the sense that they subdued and oppressed them. Just as a drunkard is senseless from drink and incapacitated, so the figure here is of the frustration and helplessness of a conquered people, powerless under the stupefying and paralysing effects of a great catastrophe (cf. Nahum 3:11).

'Pouring it from the wineskin' may be understood as mixing or adding wrath to the wine poured out, or as pouring out the wine from skins of wrath. Rather than denoting the open violence of the Babylonians, it depicts the cunning with which they deceived and overpowered their enemies.

To 'gaze on their naked bodies' is the reason behind these artifices. An ancient form of punishment was to exhibit a prisoner or criminal naked. Such an act was a public and malicious humiliation (cf. Genesis 9:21–25; Nahum 3:5; Isaiah 47:3). Here it is a figure of the shame and vulnerability of a defeated and demoralized nation. If the whole verse is interpreted literally, it possibly refers to a homosexual act.

THEIR DISGRACE (2:16)

2:16. You will be filled with shame instead of glory. Now it is your turn! Drink and be exposed! The cup from the LORD's right hand is coming around to you, and disgrace will cover your glory.

The Babylonians, especially their king, will be satiated with 'shame instead of glory'. For the time being they may pursue self-glorification through the humiliation of their neighbours; but soon, because of their shameful behaviour, they too will be humiliated; instead of glory, disgrace will return on their own heads. The phrase implies that their humiliation will be far greater than any self-assumed glory.

They have forced other nations to drink from their cup of wrath; now it is their turn to swallow the intoxicating wine of God's fury (cf. Nahum 3:11). 'Drink and be exposed!' (Babylon was captured during a drunken festival.) As they have treated others, so God will treat them. Their shame will be open for all to see; they will be exposed as an uncircumcised nation. The words 'be exposed' could be translated 'stagger'. The former corresponds well with the crime; the latter more appropriately fits the figure of drinking.

'The cup from the LORD's right hand' (cf. Psalm 75:8) is the goblet that contains God's wrath and judgement (cf. Isaiah 51:17, 22; Ezekiel 23:33) and that has been delivered by the Babylonians to the nations of the world. 'Babylon was a gold cup in the LORD's hand; she made the whole earth drunk. The nations drank her wine; therefore they have now gone mad' (Jeremiah 51:7; cf. 51:20–23; 25:15ff.). But now it is the turn of the Babylonians; they are next in line, for the cup of God's wrath is 'coming round to you'. The LORD himself, who will force them to drain it to the very dregs, is carrying it to them.

The word 'disgrace' is used only here in the Old Testament. It signifies the greatest possible contempt and means putrid shame or shameful vomit. The picture is of the Babylonians, as an object of horror and ridicule, ejecting all they have swallowed and of lying on the floor in their own vomit, drunk and naked. This vomited shame will cover their 'glory'. The word 'disgrace' could also apply to their enemies, who will spew in their faces.

THEIR VIOLENCE AND TERROR (2:17)

2:17. The violence you have done to Lebanon will overwhelm you, and your destruction of animals will terrify you. For you have shed man's blood; you have destroyed lands and cities and everyone in them.

'Lebanon' is a beautiful and fruitful mountain range in Syria, well known for its lush vegetation and mighty cedars (cf. Psalm 72:16; Hosea 14:5–7). Some interpret it figuratively and say it represents either the inhabitants, the beauty and glory of the Holy Land (cf. Deuteronomy 3:25; Jeremiah 22:6, 23), or the temple in Jerusalem, which was built from the cedars of Lebanon.

'The violence you have done to Lebanon', according to the symbolic view, describes the systematic rape and devastation of Israel (and the temple) by the Babylonians. The literalists, on the other hand, point to the ravages of the Babylonian soldiers, who have destroyed Lebanon's beauty by cutting down cedars for their own military operations and building programme.

The Babylonians will 'overwhelm' or devastate themselves with their own violence; they will crush themselves, as it were, under a cedar roof. The word 'overwhelm' may even picture the cedars of Lebanon deliberately falling on the fleeing and terrified soldiers. Again the punishment fits the crime. They will reap what they have sown. Reciprocal justice is often God's way of chastising the sinner.

The phrase 'and your destruction of animals' either denotes the Babylonians' slaughter of the animals that once inhabited the forest of Lebanon; the inhabitants of Israel or Lebanon, who have been destroyed in an animal-like fashion by the Babylonians; the enemies of the Babylonians, devouring them as wild animals devour their prey; or simply that the Babylonians are beasts without a future. The first view is the most suitable. The Babylonians have dealt savagely with all parts of creation, animate and inanimate, devastating both plant and animal life.

The animals (or men) that the Babylonians have destroyed will return to 'terrify' them. Perhaps the Babylonians will be terrified by a vision of these slaughtered beasts.

Those who understand 'Lebanon' to represent the land of Canaan and 'animals' to depict men argue that the 'destruction of animals' corresponds to the 'shedding of man's blood' and the 'violence … done to Lebanon' parallels with 'destroying lands and cities and everyone in them' (cf. 2:8).

A few summarize the first half of the verse by saying, not satisfied with robbing men and nations and with oppressing and ill-treating them, the Babylonians committed wickedness upon the cedars and cypresses also and the wild animals of Lebanon, cutting down the wood either for military purposes or for state buildings, so that the wild animals were unsparingly exterminated and terrified by the devastation.

The fifth woe against the Babylonians (2:18–20)

The final 'woe' differs from the other four in that the 'woe' is not at the beginning; instead the first verse (18) is preliminary, preparing the way for the 'woe' that opens the second verse (19). It has been suggested that Habakkuk changes the order of the oracle simply as a literary device to provide variety and climax in his expression.

Although verse 18 is a denunciation, there is, within the whole oracle, no mention of a specific judgement. However, the guilt and impending destruction of the Babylonians are clearly attributed to idol-worship; in fact, idolatry (cf. 1:16) was probably the source of all their other evils. The prophet derides these lifeless and useless images and stresses the vanity of the confidence that the Babylonians show in them; for no one can stand against the true God, the supreme ruler and only governor of the world.

THEIR IDOLATRY (2:18–19)

2:18. Of what value is an idol, since a man has carved it? Or an image that teaches lies? For he who makes it trusts in his own creation; he makes idols that cannot speak.

An 'idol', carved from dead materials such as wood and stone, is unworthy of trust and without profit; for it has been shaped by 'a man' in the image of his own depraved and corrupt nature. He knows how it was formed and from what it was made and how easily it is destroyed; its lifeless nature he cannot change. What folly it is for a man to worship a helpless block of wood or a lump of stone! 'All who make idols are nothing, and the things they treasure are worthless' (Isaiah 44:9ff.; cf. 45:20; Jeremiah 2:11).

An 'image' is made from gold or silver or some other precious metal. It is first melted, then moulded (cf. Exodus 32:4,8). It 'teaches lies' (cf. Jeremiah 10:8,14) in the sense that it withdraws the mind from the true God and deceives both men and women into trusting it for blessing and salvation; its external appearance deludes the onlooker with an impression of power. It is a false object of worship that, in contrast to God, cannot teach the truth. The phrase could also apply to the false prophets and priests, who speak on its behalf, encouraging others to make and worship man-made images.

'He who makes it' knows there is no life, strength or wisdom in it, and yet he still 'trusts' it. How foolish! For what is made is always inferior to the maker; it possesses no quality other than what has been given to it by its designer. He who places the hope of his soul in his 'own creation' defies reason and is classed as a fool.

He makes 'idols that cannot speak' or literally 'dumb nothings', or as someone else has put it, 'dumb dummies'. These idols are used in divination and consulted for oracles of wisdom and yet they have no power. They give no answers or guidance, offer no advice, make no promises, utter no threats; they are in every sense dumb.

Such idols are described by the Psalmist: 'They have mouths, but cannot speak, eyes, but they cannot see; they have ears, but cannot hear, noses, but they cannot smell; they have hands, but cannot feel, feet, but they cannot walk; nor can they utter a sound with their throats. Those who make them will be like them, and so will all who trust in them' (115:5–8).

2:19. Woe to him who says to wood, 'Come to life!' Or to lifeless stone, 'Wake up!' Can it give guidance? It is covered with gold and silver; there is no breath in it.

After deriding 'idols that cannot speak' (v.18), the LORD mocks and threatens the men who put their trust in them. 'Woe to him who says' to a worthless log, 'Come to life!' (cf. Jeremiah 2:27; Hosea 4:12). Does a dead god hear and respond to the idolater's cry? 'Woe to him who says ... to lifeless stone, "Wake up!"' Is the idol asleep that it needs to be stirred? (cf. 1 Kings 18:26–29). 'Wake up!' is a form of prayer that men often use when imploring the true God for help (cf. Psalm 35:23; Isaiah 51:9).

'Can it give guidance?' is a question of astonishment. Is it possible for a dumb and dead idol to direct others, for it to give the counsel and advice that belong only to God? It is but a teacher of lies (v.18) that is 'covered with gold and silver' (cf. Psalm 135:15–17). The word 'covered' literally means 'held fast' and often depicts idols that are fastened to pedestals by gold and silver chains. Here it means that the idol is encased in gold and silver. (The Babylonians were renowned for the lavish use of silver and gold in their temples.)

The idol might look beautiful on the outside, but it is a mask. Under the precious metals lies an object that has 'no breath in it' (cf. Jeremiah 10:14); it is lifeless and therefore owns no soul, no feelings, no understanding, no spirit. How then can it give guidance?

THE LIVING AND HOLY GOD (2:20)
2:20. But the LORD is in his holy temple; let all the earth be silent before him.

Here the contrast is drawn between the dead and dumb idols of the Babylonians and the true and living God, the fountain of all life and power. He is dwelling in his 'holy temple' or the palace of his holiness. This is not a reference to the earthly temple in Jerusalem, but to the heavenly abode of God, who sits in transcendent majesty. From there he sees, hears and saves his chosen people; from there he governs and judges the nations of the world (cf. Psalm 11:4; Isaiah 6:1–4; Micah 1:2); from there he manifests his holiness and sovereign power in the destruction of his enemies.

Let every nation 'be silent before him' (cf. Zephaniah 1:7; Zechariah 2:13). The implication is that God is about to judge the nations of the world, revealing himself as the Holy One; therefore let his enemies stand back in fear and awe and be hushed, and let his people quietly submit to his will and wait patiently for his judgement. He is a God of justice, truth and power; for this reason let 'all the earth', as a mark of reverence and dependency, be still in his presence (cf. Psalm 46:10; Isaiah 41:1).

On the one hand, dead idols 'cannot speak' (2:18) because of their impotency; on the other, the inhabitants of the world are bidden to keep 'silent' because of God's majesty and power.

Habakkuk's prayer (3:1–19)

Habakkuk responds to God as spokesman for the whole community. He offers a poetic psalm or prayer in which he glorifies God for his person (vv. 2–3b,4) and for his actions in creation (vv. 3a,5–15), and which was probably designed for public recitation in the temple as part of Israel's worship of God. The chapter concludes with a moving and powerful declaration of faith (vv. 16–19). Faith triumphs in life by the intervening power of God.

Title and introduction (3:1)

3:1. A prayer of Habakkuk the prophet. On shigionoth .

Habakkuk's dialogue with God has ended. The prophet now turns to prayer. The title 'a prayer' is an expression that occurs mainly in the psalms of lament, where intercession is made for divine intervention and vindication against oppression or injustice. In fact, it is attributed to five psalms of lament or petition (Psalms 17; 86; 90; 102; 142; cf. 72:20). It may even be a general name for a song of worship or a hymn of praise. The 'prayer' includes supplication and thanksgiving and may have been offered by Habakkuk in the temple as a prayer for his people to use.

It is a prayer 'of [or by] Habakkuk the prophet'; that is, Habakkuk, a covenantal mediator, who intercedes on behalf of his people, composed it. The term 'prophet' is also used to express the prophetical character of the prayer.

'On shigionoth' is the plural form of *shiggaion*, which occurs only in Psalm 7. It is derived from a verb meaning 'to reel to and fro' and may describe a reeling song or hymn that is sung triumphantly, with sudden changes of emotion. One commentator says it denotes a lyrical poem composed under strong mental excitement, the dithyrambic of the Greek. Another remarks that it points to the deep and violent feelings that were rolling like surging waves and billows over the prophet, tossing him backwards and forwards, until he found peace in God.

This type of song was played on a stringed instrument, possibly a harp, and led by a professional musician. 'On' means 'according to' or 'set to' the music of the psalms. There is little modern support for the expression meaning 'errors of ignorance'.

Habakkuk's awe and plea (3:2)

3:2. LORD, I have heard of your fame; I stand in awe of your deeds, O LORD. Renew them in our day, in our time make them known; in wrath remember mercy.

This is Habakkuk's response to God's revelation. 'I have heard' either a report from someone else or received an inward illumination and understanding concerning God's past deliverances and his future appearance in judgement. It probably refers back to the first two chapters, where God answers the prophet's perplexities and announces his judgements against both Israel and Babylon.

The effect of the announcement is to cause the prophet to 'stand in awe of your deeds, O LORD'. What he has heard fills him, not with the terror of the godless, but with a childlike and reverential fear of God and his amazing works (cf. 1:5). These 'deeds' point back to the working of God's sovereign power at times such as the exodus from Egypt and the destruction of his enemies in Canaan (cf. Psalm 44:2) and forward to the judgement that is to engulf first Israel and then Babylonia.

The prophet prays that the LORD will 'renew' or 'refresh and keep alive' the knowledge and experience of his past works. The revelation of

God's character and power had faded over the years, so the prophet urges him to repeat the mighty acts of deliverance that his people enjoyed long ago. He calls for fresh and public manifestations of that power and for a renewal of his works of grace. Revive your works and 'make them known' is the prophet's plea. In this way God will reveal himself to the nations and assure his people that he still cares for them.

'In our day, in our time' is difficult to interpret. It may depict either an unknown appointed time; the time between Abraham and Christ; the year of calamity allotted to Israel; or, more likely, the time between God's chastisement of Israel and his judgement of Babylon. Habakkuk wants God to fulfil his promises and to act in power as soon as possible; to cut in half the waiting time; not to delay, but to make his deeds known to the present generation in order to stimulate their faith and hope.

The word 'wrath' refers to God's displeasure against sin in general and to his just judgement of Israel and their enemies in particular. Here the prophet, probably basing his petition on Exodus 34:6–7, prays that, during and after wrath, the LORD will remember his covenant with his people and, by softening the cruelty of the Babylonians and by accelerating their overthrow, will exhibit the merciful side of his character (cf. Psalm 77:9). He wants others to see that the LORD has not forgotten mercy. Even in wrath God desires to forgive.

The theophany (3:3–15)

In the following psalm Habakkuk sees the LORD approaching in glory to judge his enemies and to redeem his people. This coming is described in the language of theophany, in which the approach and arrival of deity is pictured in terms of extraordinary natural phenomena (vv. 3–7; cf. Exodus 3:1–5; 19:16–19; 24:15–17; 1 Kings 19:11–12). He is also described as the divine warrior, who battles both against the elements and against the enemies of his people for the sake of his name and kingdom (vv. 8–15; cf. Exodus 15:1–18; Psalm 24:7–10; 68; Isaiah 34:1–

15; 51:9–10). Thus the prophet receives answers to his prayers for revelation and mercy.

HIS GLORY AND SPLENDOUR (3:3–4)

3:3. God came from Teman, the Holy One from Mount Paran. *Selah*. His glory covered the heavens and his praise filled the earth.

'God came [literally, shall come] from Teman, the Holy One from Mount Paran' (cf. Deuteronomy 33:2). Using the name 'God' (Eloah, cf. Deuteronomy 32:15,17), which designates God as the LORD and governor of the world, the prophet points back to the theophany at Mount Sinai, where God manifested himself to his people (cf. Judges 5:4–5). Just as he appeared at Mount Sinai, so he will appear again, this time to redeem Israel and punish the Babylonians. The statement depicts a future revelation of the glory of the LORD.

'Teman' was the southern part of Edom or Seir (cf. Jeremiah 49:7,20; Amos 1:11,12; Obadiah 9). It was so called after Teman, son of Eliphaz and grandson of Esau (Genesis 36:10–11), whose descendants occupied the land. 'Paran' was a large wilderness area situated between Kadesh Barnea to the north and Mount Sinai to the south and bounded by Edom to the northeast and Egypt to the southwest.

'Mount Paran' (cf. Deuteronomy 33:2) was probably located either in the rugged granite mountains west of the Gulf of Aqabah or among the desolate cliffs of the Plateau of Paran to the northwest. The two sites are mentioned, not just as the two opposed boundaries of the journeying of Israel through the desert, but to remind Israel of the Mosaic law and of a past manifestation of God's glory and deliverance.

He who comes from Teman and Mount Paran is the 'Holy One' of Israel, the sovereign LORD of the universe, who is both perfect in holiness and almighty in power (cf. 1:12–13).

'Selah' is an obscure term. It occurs seventy times in the Psalms and three times in Habakkuk (cf. 3:9,13) and is invariably found at the end of a paragraph or after some exalted or emotional statement. It is probably a musical or literary term that serves a liturgical function. It may relate to a musical direction, either for a blast of the trumpets from the priests or for the musicians to play more loudly or a note to singers to raise their voices and repeat the previous verse; it may even denote a moment of reflection, a pause for thought, while the music plays softly in the background. It is as if both singers and players announce God's glorious coming.

The 'glory' points back to the fire and storm of Mount Sinai, where Moses trembled with fear (cf. Hebrews 12:18–21). The word is often used to depict kingly authority as revealed in God's sovereignty over creation and in history. Here it signifies his boundless majesty, the full manifestation of his attributes that blanketed or overspread his eternal abode. These attributes and works of God were worthy of spontaneous 'praise' from all creation; men everywhere made him the sole object of adoration as his splendour permeated the earth (cf. 2:14).

This verse looks both ways. It looks back to the thunder and lightning, the fire and smoke, the trumpets and trembling of Mount Sinai (cf. Exodus 19:16–19); and it looks forward to a new and universal manifestation of God's rule, to another lawgiver (cf. Deuteronomy 18:15–19) who will impart the law of life, and to a new era that will culminate in the coming of the Son of Man (cf. Matthew 24:27).

3:4. His splendour was like the sunrise; rays flashed from his hand, where his power was hidden.

The word 'splendour' depicts the brightness and lustre of the outward appearance of God's being as seen by men. It is the radiance of his presence, the brilliance of the glory in which he dwells. When he appeared he emanated the purest and brightest light, for 'God is light' (1 John 1:5; cf. Psalm 104:2).

His splendour was 'like the sunrise'. Although the light that the sun emits is an inadequate representation of God's glory—he is brighter than a thousand suns—it is, as far as it goes, a suitable symbol; for it portrays the dazzling, unshadowed, spotless purity of the Holy One, who approached with the brilliance of the rising sun (cf. Job 37:21).

'Rays' may refer to the beams of light that radiate from the morning sun or to the horns or antlers of a charging beast. The latter symbolizes power and strength; the former, the glory of the divine presence (cf. Exodus 34:29–30). It is possible to combine the two meanings so that the image portrays both glory and might.

These rays flashed 'from his hand', which was at his side. The picture is not of God wielding and directing thunderbolts from heaven or of flashes of forked lightning that darted from his hand (cf. Psalm 18:12); but of God dwelling in and, as he drew near, being surrounded by a glorious and 'unimpeachable light' (1 Timothy 6:16).

In that place, where the sun-like splendour became visible, 'his power was hidden'. The brightness of his glory veiled not merely his omnipotence, but the sum total of all his attributes. The light served a double purpose: it both revealed and concealed God. Just as the brightness of the sun hides the sun itself, so, as he came, God's radiance acted as a garment that covered his almightiness and essential glory.

HIS JUDGEMENT AND POWER (3:5–7)

3:5. Plague went before him; pestilence followed his steps.

God marched forward in judgement with an army of death in front of him and behind him. The 'plague went [literally, goes] before him' as a shield-bearer (cf. 1 Samuel 17:7) and as a messenger of death. Even before the LORD arrived, the land was scarred by plague. These plagues point to the plagues that devastated Egypt (Exodus 7–12), that punished the disobedient Israelites (cf. Exodus 32:35; Numbers 14:12) and that drove out the inhabitants of Canaan; they also point forward to an impending judgement.

The word 'pestilence' (cf. Deuteronomy 32:24) literally means 'burning heat' and describes the burning fevers and deadly diseases that afflicted and overwhelmed many nations. It may, more specifically, refer to the destruction of Sennacherib's army (2 Kings 19:35). (The imagery does not portray sparks flying from the LORD's feet as they struck the earth.) This pestilence obediently 'followed his steps', like a servant, leaving behind a trail of death. Both 'plague' and 'pestilence' are personified, adding to the effect that the latter destroyed those who escaped the former.

3:6. He stood, and shook the earth; he looked, and made the nations tremble. The ancient mountains crumbled and the age-old hills collapsed. His ways are eternal.

After the LORD arrived he 'stood' still or firmly stationed himself, in order to examine the enemy. He paused before the battle, just as the wind is calm before a storm or as a chief waits for the precise moment of attack. Then he 'shook the earth'. The verb 'shook' (LXX), which means 'rocked' and 'convulsed', can also be translated 'measured'. The LORD surveyed the earth, calmly weighing the actions of men before declaring his right, as the sovereign Creator, to judge them. 'Shook' describes the effect of God's action, 'measured' the reason behind it.

He 'looked' at or scrutinized the nations with a frown on his face and anger in his eye, making them 'tremble'. The nations were struck with sudden terror and commotion at the thought of God's wrath. They were panic-stricken and thrown into emotional and physical turmoil. 'Tremble' literally means 'to move from one place to another' and describes an abrupt and violent movement; the nations shuddered or jumped with mortal fear.

'The ancient mountains' that existed from the beginning of time (Genesis 1:9), the sure and stable foundations of the earth (cf. Deuteronomy 33:15; Micah 6:2), 'crumbled' before his presence. The oldest and firmest part of creation, those seemingly immovable symbols of grandeur and security, dissolved into dust before the LORD's rebuke; they broke into innumerable pieces, as if crushed by a giant hammer. 'And the age-old hills collapsed' or prostrated themselves before the LORD (cf. Nahum 1:5; Micah 1:4). Every heap of earth, both large and small, gave way before him and sank to level plains.

There is an eschatological aspect to this verse which must not be overlooked (cf. Psalm 97:4–5; Isaiah 29:6; Joel 3:16; Zechariah 14:4; 2 Peter 3:10; Revelation 16:18–20).

Though the mountains appeared to be never changing in character and invincible in strength, only the LORD's 'ways are eternal' or 'of old'. He alone is everlasting and immutable, the stable and consistent one, who performs works of salvation throughout history. Just as he appeared at Mount Sinai (Exodus 19:16–18) and in the wilderness, so he comes again to rescue his oppressed people.

3:7. I saw the tents of Cushan in distress, the dwellings of Midian in anguish.

'I' denotes that the prophet is the speaker. He 'saw', not with his eyes, but with his mind and understanding, a prophetic vision of 'the tents of Cushan in distress'. By 'tents' Habakkuk points to the bedouin nomads who lived in them, rather than to the tents themselves.

'Cushan' is unknown outside this passage. It may refer to Cushan-Rishathaim, king of Aram Naharaim, the first oppressor of Israel, who subjugated Israel for eight years after the death of Joshua (Judges 3:8–10). It may simply be a poetic or expanded form of Cush, as Lotan is for Lot in Genesis 36:22. If that is so, it refers to Ethiopia (the land of Cush), which lies to the west of the Red Sea. Some say Cushan is an alternative name for Midian or a subgroup of the Midianites. Others identify it with Jokshan, one of Abraham's sons by Keturah (Genesis 25:2); the Kishon River (Judges 4:7) that flows through the Valley of Esdraelon; an Arabian tribe or a bedouin tribe of the Sinai peninsula (cf. Exodus 3:1). In all probability, the prophet points to the land west of the Red Sea.

The inhabitants of this land were 'in' or under 'distress'. The word 'distress' means affliction that arises from sin, particularly the sin of injustice (cf. 1:3); it is the effect of judgement. In other words, the people of Cushan were suffering under the heavy burdens that sin imposes and eating the poisoned fruit of their own iniquity.

Habakkuk saw 'the dwellings [literally, curtains] of Midian in anguish'. The Midianites ('Midian' was one of Abraham's sons by Keturah) were nomads, who lived in tents along the Arabian coast, east of the Red Sea. They were the early oppressors of Israel (Judges 6:1–2). At the thought of God's wrath they writhe in 'anguish' or tremble with fear. They remember how Gideon had destroyed their country and slaughtered their kings (Judges 7–8; Psalm 83:9–12; Isaiah 9:4) and they quake at the prospect of an old judgement being repeated.

HIS WRATH AND POWER (3:8–10)

3:8. Were you angry with the rivers, O LORD? Was your wrath against the streams? Did you rage against the sea when you rode with your horses and your victorious chariots?

Habakkuk, as if startled by the vision, turns to the LORD and, with three rhetorical questions, asks him to explain the cause of the great miracles of the past. 'Were you angry with the rivers, O LORD? Was your wrath against the streams? Did you rage against the sea ...?' (cf. Psalm 114:3,5; Nahum 1:4). The prophet recalls the dividing of the Red Sea (Exodus 14:21–22), when God opened a safe passage for the Israelites and the parting of the Jordan (Joshua 3:15–16) which occurred forty years later.

At these times God was not angry with the water, attacking it as he would an enemy; rather, both mighty acts were for the sake and deliverance of the elect.

One commentator, while agreeing that the description rests upon the two facts of the miraculous dividing of the Red Sea and the Jordan, goes on to say that it rises far above these to a description of God as the judge of the world, who can smite in his wrath not only the sea of the world, but all the rivers of the earth as well (cf. Psalm 89:9). It may also point further back to God's dominion over the waters at creation (Genesis 1:7,9).

The following metaphor is adopted from military operations. The LORD is seen as a general at the head of an army, leading the troops into battle, as a warlike hero, riding forth with his 'horses' and 'chariots' of salvation. The allusion is probably to a human army, although it could picture the LORD striding through the heavens on thunder clouds with the angelic host, who execute his sovereign purposes (cf. Psalm 18:10–12; 104:3; Isaiah 19:1). 'Horses' and 'chariots' are representative of man's strength and are associated with the parting of the Red Sea (Exodus 14:6–9,23–28; Deuteronomy 11:4; Joshua 24:6).

'Victorious chariots' should read 'chariots of salvation' or literally 'your chariots are salvation'. (The word 'salvation' [*Jeshuah*] is derived from the same root as 'Jesus'.) The LORD rode forward to conquer his enemies and to deliver from their grasp his chosen people (cf. 3:13). The mystery of judgement is salvation and the end of wrath is mercy. Once again there is an eschatological aspect to the verse (cf. Revelation 16:3–4,12).

3:9. You uncovered your bow, you called for many arrows. *Selah*. You split the earth with rivers;

This verse is so obscure and difficult to interpret that there are over a hundred different translations and emendations of it. Only the most appropriate are presented below.

The word 'bow' either depicts a single weapon of war that God carried as a warrior or it is a term that includes the sword and other weapons (cf. Psalm 7:12–13). This bow was 'uncovered' or 'naked'; that is, it was taken out of its sheath, which was usually suspended on the side of the chariot, and made ready for action. God, whose bow was taut and whose arrows were fitted to the string, stood as a man of war, ready to unveil his power and to execute vengeance on his enemies.

The verb 'called', which can also be translated 'promised' or 'declared', may point to the word of promise (oath) that was given to the Israelites in Deuteronomy 32:40–43. There God promised to 'take vengeance on my adversaries and repay those who hate me' and to 'make my arrows drunk with blood, while my sword devours flesh'.

The adjective 'many' is ambiguous. The same root in Hebrew connotes 'swearing' as well as the number 'seven'. The latter rendering points to the sevenfold volleys of arrows that the Israelites used in warfare; whereas the former is more closely connected to Deuteronomy 32:40–43. The term may even refer to the oral 'dedication' of weapons for the destruction of enemies, a concept not unknown in Israel.

The third word 'arrows', literally 'staffs' or 'spears' (cf. 3:14) describes the weapons that were taken out of their sheaths and made ready to be used as instruments of chastisement (cf. Deuteronomy 32:23; Psalm 7:13). God's judgements were as arrows upon the string (cf. Psalm 18:14; 21:12).

'You split the earth with rivers' (cf. Psalm 74:13–15; Proverbs 3:20) or as another translates it: 'You split the rivers to the earth' is an allusion either to the parting of the Red Sea, to the rock that Moses struck (Exodus 17:6; Numbers 20:11) or to the way the earth was rent at creation (Genesis 1:9) and the flood (Genesis 7:11). It points to a time when the earth trembled at God's wrath, when water burst from the deep and rushed down the sides of mountains, gouging out huge gullies with its force and breaking open the ground.

3:10. The mountains saw you and writhed. Torrents of water swept by; the deep roared and lifted its waves on high.

This verse resembles Psalm 77:16–19, where the dividing of the Red Sea is vividly portrayed. Here the prophet uses images from the past to describe the future judgement of God. The 'mountains', which are personified and which represent either the whole of nature or the most secure part of creation, 'writhed' when they became sensible of the avenger's approach and presence. The word 'writhed' expresses the intense pain of travail (cf. Isaiah 26:18) as well as the terror of being shaken by an earthquake (cf. Psalm 68:8; Deuteronomy 2:25). It is a lasting condition that brought down even the mighty mountains.

The following sentence is associated with the parting of the Red Sea (Psalm 77), which in turn points back to the flood (Genesis 7:11–12,18–20) and the waters of creation (Genesis 1:2,6–10). 'Torrents of water' denotes both a heavy downpour of rain and the resultant flooding. These inundations of water rushed by or, in the case of the Red Sea, divided to allow the fleeing Israelites to escape.

The prophet attributes a voice to the great 'deep' (cf. Job 28:14), the subterranean waters (cf. Genesis 7:11; Deuteronomy 33:13) and the depths of the seas (cf. Psalm 77:16). This mass of water in the abyss 'roared'; it emitted a dreadful, gurgling sound as its torrents burst forth uncontrollably from the earth.

'It lifted its waves on high' in obedience to God's command. As the waves swelled they were thrown up into mountainous heaps, becoming visible to all. In this way they united with the rains from heaven and broke through the floodgates of the earth (cf. Nahum 2:6). The clause draws on the imagery of waves that stretch their foaming whitecaps heavenward, reaching ever upward to enclose more of the world within their domain. Some translate 'waves' as 'hands' and picture the deep lifting up its hands in prayer as if pleading with God for mercy.

HIS SPLENDOUR AND WRATH (3:11–12)

3:11. Sun and moon stood still in the heavens at the glint of your flying arrows, at the lightning of your flashing spear.

This was nature's response to God's judgement. The 'sun and moon stood still'; that is, the celestial bodies ceased to give light. They were either enveloped and obscured by the clouds of the tempest or they hid themselves during the storm of God's wrath, withdrawing into their dwelling-places. Perhaps this obscuration was not the effect of heavy clouds that pour out their water in showers of rain, but was caused by the shining of the arrows of God; in other words, the sun and moon 'stood still' because they were terrified of God's judgement. Either way, the order of creation was interrupted and darkness was allowed to rule. (Darkness is often the sign of God's presence and judgement [cf. Deuteronomy 4:11; Psalm 18:11; Joel 2:31].) The 'heavens' is an exalted tabernacle or heavenly abode into which the sun and moon withdrew.

There is probably not a direct reference to Joshua 10:12–13 in this verse, although the prophet may well have that extraordinary event in the back of his mind. The two episodes can be contrasted, however: in Joshua the sun and moon stood still to give light to the avengers; in Habakkuk both stood in awe and terror, overpowered by the terrific splendour of God's light.

The sun and moon hid themselves at the sight of God's 'flying arrows' and 'flashing spear' (cf. Nahum 3:3), driven away by the light of divine splendour that shone from the metal heads and polished shafts. These instruments of judgement (cf. Psalm 18:14; 77:17; Zechariah 9:14), hurled by God's mighty hand, flew through the darkness like bolts of lightning or as a devouring fire (cf. Isaiah 10:17), certain to reach their target. This sort of deadly 'lightning' occurs in theophanies and acts of judgement.

3:12. In wrath you strode through the earth and in anger you threshed the nations.

Although the prophet draws on the past history of Israel, it is the present and future that he has in mind; for in this and the following verses he portrays the immediate and final objects of God's judgement. The LORD approached in awesome glory and in avenging 'wrath' (indignation against sin). The verb 'strode' depicts the LORD as an all-conquering warrior, marching into battle to destroy the enemy (cf. Judges 5:4; Psalm 68:7–8). Under the weight and at the sound of his footsteps the 'earth' trembled.

Just as he did at the exodus and during the conquest of Canaan, so will he 'thresh' the heathen 'nations' that oppose Israel. Foreigners will again feel his presence and anger as he stamps on them, trampling them underfoot. 'Threshed' denotes the violent shaking and crushing that smashed the nations into pieces (cf. Micah 4:13; Psalm 68:21; Isaiah 21:10).

HIS SALVATION AND JUDGEMENT (3:13–14)

3:13. You came out to deliver your people, to save your anointed one. You crushed the leader of the land of wickedness, you stripped him from head to foot. Selah.

Here the prophet reverts to the past as a pledge and assurance of the future; or, to put it another way, he describes the future by referring to the past. The LORD, as a divine warrior, marched out to war ('came out') in order to 'deliver' or rescue his chosen 'people'; he fought on their behalf (cf. 2 Samuel 5:24; Isaiah 42:13).

This part of the verse not only points to God's special, covenant relationship with his elect (he remembers his covenant and therefore acts on Israel's behalf); it also answers the prophet's complaint (1:12–17), assuring him that Israel's salvation, which started with the exodus and continued through the wilderness into the promised land, will be completed.

Habakkuk repeats the message of salvation in order to emphasize the great mercy of God. 'To save your anointed one [Messiah]' can also be translated: 'For salvation with your anointed one,' making the Messiah actively involved in the accomplishment of this work of salvation. The former translation is to be preferred, however.

There are various interpretations as to the identity of the 'anointed one'. It certainly does not point to all Israel, as the text is singular and the nation of Israel is never referred to in the Old Testament as the anointed of the LORD.

The title may depict an individual, possibly one of the kings of Judah, who here represents the faithful in Israel and who foreshadows the Christ. Maybe it is the divinely-anointed king of Israel; that is, not this or that historical king, but the Davidic king absolutely, including the Messiah, in whom the sovereignty of David is raised to an eternal duration. In other words, it points to the Davidic king as the head of the theocracy and as a type of the Messiah. Perhaps the 'anointed one' represents both the king in Habakkuk's own time and the Christ, whose sufferings and glory the prophets predicted (1 Peter 1:10–12). Other less tenable interpretations include Joshua, Moses and even Cyrus.

The word 'crushed' means 'pierced, dashed to pieces, inflicted with a deadly wound' (cf. Genesis 3:15; Psalm 68:21; 110:5). The 'leader' or head (chief) probably refers to the Babylonian king and his empire, although it could point to Pharaoh and the kings and princes of Canaan before the conquest (cf. Psalm 110:6).

Some understand 'leader' to mean the 'roof' of a house. This interpretation fits in well with the word 'land' (settlements), which can also be translated 'house'. If this is correct, the enemy is portrayed as a building whose roof was smashed (and whose walls collapsed as a result), leaving the inhabitants exposed and unprotected. 'Wickedness' or 'the wicked one' points either to the king of Babylon, his wicked subjects and ungodly kingdom or to the leaders before and after the exodus.

'You stripped him from head to foot' either compares the enemy to a human body or continues the building analogy. The former depicts the complete uncovering and thorough humiliation of 'the wicked one'; he was laid bare for all to see (cf. Isaiah 47:3; Lamentations 4:21; Ezekiel 16:37). The latter describes the entire demolition of a house; the whole structure was razed to the ground and not one brick was left on top of another. This second interpretation is possible because 'foot' means 'foundation' and 'head' refers to the gable of a roof.

One commentator applies this verse to Christ's victory over Satan. He remarks that the warfare between these two adversaries culminated in the great battle on Golgotha, which ended in Satan's complete and everlasting defeat and in the full and eternal salvation of God's elect. There the head of the house of the wicked received his mortal wound.

3:14. With his own spear you pierced his head when his warriors stormed out to scatter us, gloating as though about to devour the wretched who were in hiding.

The role of victor/victim is suddenly reversed under the power of God, for 'with his own spear you pierced his head'. 'Pierced' has a similar meaning to 'crushed' (3:13) and may allude to Judges 5:26. 'Head' is similar to 'leader' (3:13), except in this verse it includes all the attacking hordes. The destruction that 'the wicked one' had prepared for others, came on himself; with their own weapons, the marauders destroyed themselves (cf. Obadiah 15). There may be a reference here to the fall of Babylon by Cyrus; for that city fell without a fight, its 'leader' being betrayed by factions among his own subjects.

This self-destruction occurred when the warlike troops 'stormed out' (cf. 1:9,11) against God's people. Their approach was as swift and as violent as a tempest and as destructive as a whirlwind. Their intention was 'to scatter us' like chaff in the wind (cf. Isaiah 41:16; Jeremiah 13:24) and to drive us from the earth (cf. Exodus 14:5–10). The 'us' or 'me' refers to Habakkuk either as a member of the community or as the people's spokesman and representative.

The enemy approached, exulting gleefully in their success and rejoicing in the spoils and victory of war (cf. 1:15–16); they were like wild and hungry animals as they assaulted and murdered their prey (cf. 1:8; 2:5). The 'wretched' were the poor, defenceless and oppressed people of Israel. 'In hiding' may refer to their attempt to protect themselves from the attackers; or, and this is more likely, it points to the attackers, who were hoping 'to devour the wretched' in secret. This alludes to the practice of wild beasts that drag their prey into dens before devouring it. One commentator compares the enemy to highway murderers, who lurk in dark corners for the defenceless traveller and look forward with rejoicing for the moment when they may be able to murder him (cf. Psalm 10:8–11).

HIS POWER (3:15)

3:15. You trampled the sea with your horses, churning the great waters.

This verse is similar to 3:8 and alludes to the crossing of the Red Sea. It describes the kind of power that enables God to save the righteous and destroy the wicked. With his 'horses' harnessed to chariots, he 'trampled' or walked on/through 'the sea'. Just as he passed through the sea to complete the Israelites escape from Egypt (Psalm 77:19), so he will come again to rescue his people from Babylon. No obstacle will hinder his progress; no army will thwart his purpose. It is interesting to note that Babylon's destruction (539 BC) was brought about by the enemy's entrance along the dried-up river bed of the Euphrates.

As God's horses charge through the sea they 'churn' up the 'great waters' all around them, just as a marching army raises a dust cloud or as a storm stirs the sea. The word 'churning', which is derived from a verb meaning 'to ferment', may signify 'heap' (cf. Exodus 15:8). This interpretation strengthens the allusion to the parting of the Red Sea (cf. Psalm 78:13). The 'great waters' could also refer to a host of enemies or even to the subjugation of the Canaanites.

Habakkuk's faith (3:16–19b)

God answers Habakkuk's complaints so thoroughly and with such a powerful vision that the prophet is left in a state of exhaustion and stunned awe. Trembling and yet with a sense of overwhelming joy, he describes the feelings that are produced within himself by the coming of the LORD to judge the nations and to rescue his own people. The result is one of the most moving statements of faith found anywhere in the Bible.

HIS FEAR AND PATIENCE (3:16)

3:16. I heard and my heart pounded, my lips quivered at the sound; decay crept into my bones, and my legs trembled. Yet I will wait patiently for the day of calamity to come on the nation invading us.

The opening of this verse is similar to 3:2. 'I heard' may refer to 3:3–15, but more probably it points back to the description of the 'ruthless and impetuous' Babylonians and their invasion of Judah (1:5–11). At the prospect of this judgement Habakkuk's whole being is shaken emotionally, mentally and physically.

His 'heart pounded'. The Hebrews regard the 'heart' or belly (lower abdomen) as the seat of the emotions, the innermost part of an individual (cf. Proverbs 20:27; Isaiah 16:11). Habakkuk's heart 'pounded' or trembled with fear and astonishment. His whole inward self vibrated at the thought of God's wrath. He was torn by spasms, overpowered by feelings of dismay, terrified with forebodings. His 'lips' palpitated or chattered like teeth to such an extent that he could hardly fulfil the prophetic office and utter the terrors he heard.

The strongest part of his body ('my bones') was smitten with a rottenness that consumed his strength and languished his spirits (cf. Proverbs 12:4; 14:30). An uncontrollable weakness seemed to sap his vigour. His 'legs [lower limbs] trembled' as if shaken by an earthquake. He could only totter and not properly support himself. He was ready to collapse. From top to bottom he was convulsed by terror.

Some commentators understand the following sentence to mean that Habakkuk will wait quietly for God to pour out his wrath on Israel, for the inevitable assault of Babylon's invading armies. However, in view of the extraordinary faith he displays in verse 17, it is more likely that the prophet 'will wait patiently for the day of calamity to come on the nation [Babylon] invading' Israel. In other words, with the eyes of faith, he sees beyond Israel's judgement to the destruction of Babylon, which occurred in 539 BC at the hands of the Medes and Persians.

Habakkuk realizes his own powerlessness to avert Israel's punishment, so he will silently submit to God, trusting him to bring salvation to his people in his own time. The 'day of calamity' is the day of God's wrath against Israel's enemies; it is a time of deep distress from which there will be no deliverance. The 'nation invading us' may allude to 2 Kings 24:2, where hostile troops were sent against Jehoiakim after his rebellion; or it may, more specifically, depict the actual fall of Jerusalem in Zedekiah's time (2 Kings 25).

HIS AFFLICTION AND JOY (3:17–18)

3:17. Though the fig tree does not bud and there are no grapes on the vines, though the olive crop fails and the fields produce no food, though there are no sheep in the pen and no cattle in the stalls …

The basis of Israel's agricultural economy was the produce of their crops and livestock. During the war with the Babylonians both plants and animals are destroyed (cf. Jeremiah 5:17), leaving the land in the grip of famine and the economy devastated. By referring to the ravages of war, the prophet is reminding his people of the natural and military disasters that overtake all who disobey God's covenant (cf. Leviticus 26:20,22,25–26; Deuteronomy 11:17).

The 'fig-tree, vines and olives' are mentioned as the choicest products of the land (cf. Hosea 2:12; Micah 4:4; 6:15). The 'fig tree' shows no sign of bearing fruit (perhaps it has been cut down); the 'vines' are stripped bare by the invaders; the 'olive crop' disappoints and frustrates the expectations of both sower and reaper (cf. Hosea 9:2). Here the prophet numbers from the least to the greatest the fruits of the trees and portrays the well-being of the vine and the fig tree as a proverbial picture of peace and rest.

The cornfields that were ploughed and sown are trampled by the enemy and so produce no grain; the 'sheep' that are usually enclosed safely in their pens and the 'cattle', though locked in their 'stalls', are both carried away by the Babylonians. At the hands of the spoilers the people of God suffer the loss of all things. In other words, there are no fig cakes, no wine, no anointing oil, no cereal, no vegetables, no milk, no mutton, no wool left in the land for the people to enjoy. Not only the prosperity, but the very life of the nation fails and is cut off.

3:18. … yet I will rejoice in the LORD, I will be joyful in God my Saviour.

Despite the calamities that devastate both the land and economy of Israel, the prophet will fix his eyes on God, the only true object of faith, and trust him to accomplish his purpose. He will see, not the works of God, but God himself. He will find his salvation, not in material prosperity, but in the giver and sustainer of life. God will be his inexhaustible source and infinite sphere of joy. By the grace of God the complainer becomes the rejoicer.

Commentary

'Yet [nevertheless] I will rejoice' (cf. 3:16b; Micah 7:7). Such exultation and deep emotion is reminiscent of the psalmists, who often expressed strong faith and joy in God (cf. Isaiah 25:9) during seasons of severe affliction (cf. Hebrews 12:2). Habakkuk's joy springs from his close relationship with God and from his personal knowledge of and faith in his unchangeable Word. He will rejoice 'in the LORD' (cf. Psalm 32:11), not in victories over the enemy (cf. Babylonians 1:10–11; 3:14), not in outward prosperity, comforts and blessing, but in the person and promises of his Saviour.

The prophet renews and confirms his faith when he declares, 'I will be joyful in God my Saviour.' He calls God his own and promises to rejoice in him who, despite Israel's impending judgement, is still 'my Saviour' from times of distress (cf. 3:13). Salvation from an Old Testament perspective includes all the material blessings that life can offer, along with the wholeness of a soul united to God.

Salvation will result from the present disaster, for judgement is the stepping-stone to mercy for the elect; in wrath God remembers mercy. The same covenant that threatens the disobedient with destruction and exile also promises restoration and prosperity to all who return to the LORD (Leviticus 26; Deuteronomy 28). It is on these covenantal promises that the prophet's hope and joy are founded.

HIS CONFIDENCE AND VICTORY (3:19A–B)

3:19a. The Sovereign LORD is my strength;

The final verse is borrowed from Psalm 18 (vv. 32–33), a Davidic hymn of triumph. 'The Sovereign LORD [Israel's God] is my strength,' declares the prophet. This statement echoes the song of Moses (Exodus 15:2,13) and shows why Habakkuk will rejoice in times of tribulation. All might and confidence come from God alone, who sustains the prophet by his power and upholds him in the storms of life.

3:19b. he makes my feet like the feet of a deer, he enables me to go on the heights.

'He makes my feet like the feet of a deer' (cf. 2 Samuel 22:34; Psalm 18:33). Some are inclined to refer this to Israel's return to their own country, although they admit another explanation: God will give the swiftest feet to his servants, so that they may pass over all obstacles to destroy their enemies. Others think it is a figure for the irresistible strength that springs from confidence in God.

The simile probably reflects the grace, sure-footedness and vitality of the deer as it prances and leaps from crag to crag without slipping. This in turn reflects Habakkuk's joy and confidence in God. Before his 'legs trembled' (3:16), now his feet dance. It is as if his people, of whom he is the representative, as they trust in the providence of God, bound upwards with renewed youthfulness, springing into the safe hands of the sovereign LORD. In battle their feet do not slip and their hands never grow tired as they swiftly destroy their enemies.

'He enables me to go on the heights' (cf. 2 Samuel 22:34; Psalm 18:33) of victory. The word 'heights' does not refer to the mountains of Israel, but to the place of conquest and domain, to the high places of salvation that are climbed only by faith (cf. 2:4). It denotes the ultimate triumph of the people of God over all oppression. The clause points back to Deuteronomy 32:13 and 33:29, where in both cases the context is the joyful conquest and possession of the land.

The subscription (3:19c)

3:19c. For the director of music. On my stringed instruments.

'For the director of music' occurs fifty-five times in the Psalms. Here it refers back to 3:1, suggesting that the whole chapter was used in the temple as part of the liturgical and public worship of God. It may be that the prophet wants his faith, hope and joy to be a pattern for other generations to follow and celebrate. The 'director of music' is the conductor of the temple choir, who sang psalms in the temple services.

These psalms are accompanied by 'stringed instruments' (cf. Isaiah 38:20), elsewhere translated 'song' (Job 30:9) or 'music' (Lamentations 5:14). It probably refers to the zither, one of the instruments used by the Levites to accompany the hymns sung by the temple choir. It may have been played by Habakkuk himself, which supports the idea that the prophet was a member of the Levitical choir, perhaps one of the chorus leaders.

On this note of triumph and confident rejoicing, Habakkuk's remarkable psalm ends. It was written not only as a private memorial of his conflicting emotions, but as an encouragement for his fellow believers, who were suffering the same perplexities as his own.